WILDLIFE
SPECIALS

Published by Trident Press Ltd.
2-5 Old Bond Street, London W1X 3TB
Tel: 0171 491 8770 Fax: 0171 491 8664 E-mail: tridentp@iol.ie
Internet: http://www.tridentpress.com

Layout & Design © 1997: Trident Press Ltd.

Editor: Keith Scholey, BBC Natural History Unit
Picture Research: Helen Gilks, BBC N.H.U. Picture Library

Publishing Director: Peter Vine
General Editor: Paula Vine
Copy Editor: Gabrielle Warnock
Typesetting and design: Johan Hofsteenge
Cover consultant: Megan Vine

Photographs: The publishers are pleased to acknowledge and
thank the BBC Natural History Unit Picture Library for access
to its extensive collection of wildlife photographs. It also
acknowledges with thanks the additional picture agencies and
individual photographers whose photographs are credited on
their relevant pages.

Cover photographs: main picture of humpback whales lunge
feeding: Brandon D. Cole, leopard: Anup Shah, humpback
whale: Brandon D. Cole, hatchling crocodile: Bruce Davidson
(Oxford Scientific Films), golden eagle: John Downer, wolf: Tom
Vezo. Leopard on half-title page: Owen Newman, polar bear on
pages 2 and 3: Thomas D. Mangelsen, crocodile on page 6:
Richard Du Toit.

Printed on 100% chlorine free paper by Emirates Printing Press,
Dubai, United Arab Emirates.

Distribution: Biblios Book Publishers Distribution Services Ltd.,
Star Road, Partridge Green, West Sussex RH13 8DL, UK
Tel: 01403 710851; Fax: 01403 711143

British Library Cataloguing in Publication Data
A CIP catalogue record for this book is available from the British
Library.

ISBN: 1-900724-16-2

THE BBC NATURAL HISTORY UNIT'S

WILDLIFE SPECIALS

TRIDENT
PRESS

Contents

Foreword

PROVIDING THE COMMENTARY for a natural history film can be a salutary business. It is done by sitting in front of a television screen running the pictures backwards and forwards as you grope for the words - not too many, not too few - that will provide that little bit of necessary information that the pictures cannot convey by themselves. But if you were alongside the cameraman when he was shooting, and especially if you had some hand in shaping the film's construction, then your spirits begin to sink. As you run the sequences for the thirtieth or fortieth time, the shots that you thought were so thrilling when you first saw them, seem less exciting. Do they really convey the excitement of what you saw? And what about those things that you didn't see, the things that some expert told you that the animal did - but the animals themselves didn't seem to know about and certainly never did while you were there? And that story line that you helped construct - isn't it really sadly predictable and totally lacking in suspense? For me, this is the really low point in film-making.

But if you haven't been involved in the shooting of the film - and I wasn't in all those that are described in this book - then commentary writing is an exciting and thought provoking time. Often you see things that you have never seen before and to provide the right words for them you must discover from those that were there the background to what the camera recorded. And as you go through the film again and again and these outstanding shots become more familiar, questions about much of the rest begin to form in your mind. How on earth did Martha and Martin get so close to those notoriously dangerous animals the polar bears? How could they have

David Attenborough with wandering albatross chick on South Georgia.

defended themselves if the animals had become aggressive? Did Richard really jump in the river alongside those crocodiles? If he didn't how did he get the pictures and if he did how did he survive? How long did Mike and Jeff have to follow that pack of hunting wolves before they could get alongside the animals as they closed in on their prey? Where did they sleep? How did they travel? What did they eat? In short, how on earth, in practical terms, were they in the right place with a camera on a tripod and running, at exactly the right time?

The questions keep occurring to you. If you ask the cameraman and directors who came back with these pictures, they tend to say that they were lucky. Perhaps that is true. But I know that such people make their own luck. And I have an idea about their recipe. The ingredients include such a deep knowledge and empathy with animals that you know what one is going to do before it does it, an ability to take a camera to pieces on a cloth spread on a cabin table while your boat is pitching in heavy seas, lateral thinking, a capacity to disregard the taste of particularly disagreeable food and think of it merely as essential fuel, bravery, irrepressible good humour under dreadful discomfort, physical strength, a wholly enviable skill at sweet talking officials of all kinds in an airport, an ability to laugh at your companion's stories when told for the umpteenth time for the benefit of a stranger, and an inextinguishable determination never to give up. Some of that may be obvious from the words on the following pages. The rest, and much more besides, you will detect if you read between the lines.

David Attenborough

The Wildlife Specials

KEITH SCHOLEY

IN OCTOBER 1995 the then controller of BBC 1, Alan Yentob, gave the go-ahead for one of the most challenging projects the BBC Natural History Unit had ever undertaken, *The Wildlife Specials*. These were to be six films that would provide new insight into some of the world's most famous and charismatic animals. In doing so they would present the most detailed portrait possible of each chosen species' life. The 'film-stars' were to be the polar bear, the

*Series Producer of
The Wildlife Specials,
Keith Scholey.*

wolf, the crocodile, the leopard, the eagle and the humpback whale. The idea was intoxicating; turning it into reality proved to be more demanding than any of us had imagined. It is an unfortunate fact that famous and charismatic animals tend to be rare, elusive and dangerous and therefore extremely difficult to film. Our selected subjects were no exceptions.

The reader may be forgiven for assuming that, after some 40 years of wildlife film-making, there would be little left to reveal about animals as renowned as these. In reality, however, there was considerable scope for filming previously unrecorded aspects of all their lives - simply because doing so had always been so taxing in the past. For the ambitious wildlife film-maker greater achievements still were within reach. However, the risk of failure was equally large. Filming wild animals is a hazardous undertaking and quite unpredictable in its results. Unlike their comrades in other fields of programme-making, wildlife film-makers have little or no control over their subjects and it is the animals themselves that must tell the story. There is always a risk that the anticipated players will not put in an appearance during the entire filming period and when they do appear, the chances that they will perform in front of the camera are slim. It is not unusual for a filming team to return from an arduous and expensive trip with nothing of any worth to show for their efforts. This happens with depressing regularity even in pursuit of the most commonplace animals. So any film which is expected to display previously unrecorded behaviour by a rare animal courts an alarmingly high possibility of failure.

While we were all delighted that Alan Yentob had shown so much faith in us by commissioning *The Wildlife Specials*, we also knew that we had let ourselves in for a demanding and nerve-wracking project. The basis for this formidably hazardous series was the past experience of the Natural History Unit. We had previously tackled elusive subjects in many different parts of the world. The Unit 's origins were

JOHN SPARKS

David Attenborough with mountain gorillas during the filming of Life on Earth.

in radio, starting with two experimental radio broadcasts back in 1946. By 1957 the Natural History Unit was formally established, with television programmes comprising part of its output. From this very small beginning it has grown to become the world's leading production centre of wildlife films. Wildlife presenters such as David Attenborough, Gerald Durrell, Desmond Morris and David Bellamy have become household names, and long running series like *Wildlife on One* and *The Natural World* have reached audiences of many millions around the world. David Attenborough's major works, such as *Life on Earth*, *The Living Planet*, *The Trials of Life* and *The Private Life of Plants*, have become television classics. Today the Natural History Unit consists of some 200 people and works with wildlife film makers all over the world.

The size and experience of the Unit make it unique. From its early days it has always attracted people with a passion for wild animals and places, and a drive to reveal more and more about the natural world. Over the years these presenters, researchers, producers, and camera operators have worked closely together to find new ways of filming wildlife. The existence of this large and close-knit group has allowed ideas and techniques to be shared, refined and embellished. The result has been increasingly challenging projects, both to satisfy the film-makers' ambitions, and to try to keep pace with the rising expectations of audiences world-wide.

Peter Scott, director of the Severn Wildfowl Trust, at Slimbridge during the broadcast of The Naturalist; Wild Geese, broadcast on 4 January 1947. The interviewer is Desmond Hawkins.

Gerald Durrell with 'Lu-Lu', the young chimpanzee from his zoo in Jersey, photographed in 1961, during filming of Zoo Packet.

Hans and Lotte Hass in diving gear during the filming of Diving to Adventure in 1958.

Gerald Durrell, who introduced To Bafut for Beef, together with his chimpanzee Cholmondley St. John, during a rehearsal break in the studio, in April 1958.

*Armand and Michaela Dennis
filming their* Safari to Asia
series, in Japan, 1960.

*Michaela Dennis with pet
chimpanzee Charlie, from the
filming of* On Safari, *July 1961.*

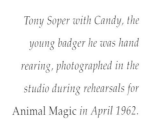

*Tony Soper with Candy, the
young badger he was hand
rearing, photographed in the
studio during rehearsals for*
Animal Magic *in April 1962.*

Eric Ashby, one of the first 'great' natural history photographers, at work in the early 1960's, adjusting one of his cameras mounted in a wooden box to absorb camera noise. Ashby's films of foxes and badgers, much of which were shot in black and white, remain classics among wildlife films.

David Attenborough and Peter Scott during Guest at Slimbridge in May 1962.

Gerald Durrell and his assistant, John Hartley, examine some new arrivals to their animal collection at Bambawo, Sierra Leone. Waiting to film them are Christopher Parsons (director), Ewart Needham (cameraman) and Howard Smith (recordist). The resulting film, Catch Me a Colubus, was shown on BBC 1 in 1966.

Dr Desmond Morris (left) and
Dr Jan van Hooff with a
macaque monkey during the
BBC 2 programme Life in
November 1965.

Johnny Morris and white
tiger cub in studio, 1974.

David Attenborough at the edge
of the Grand Canyon during
filming of Life on Earth.

Great-white shark off southern Australia.

This was the creative and challenging atmosphere which fostered the first 'Wildlife Special' and its continuance has led, in turn, to the present series. The original 'Special' was a film about the most infamous fish in the ocean, the great-white shark. Prior to that programme, all that had been shown of the marine giant were wild sharks drawn by bait to underwater cameramen in protective cages (and, of course, those monstrous, great-white Hollywood robots!). No natural behaviour had ever been filmed. This is not surprising as great-whites are very rare indeed and had not even been filmed underwater until the end of the 1960s. Even trying to bait the sharks close to cages is difficult and few have succeeded in doing it. So, until the late 1980s, no one in their right mind would ever have proposed making a film about their wild behaviour. This all changed when a producer in the Natural History Unit, Michael Bright, learned of an interesting piece of research being carried out on California's Farallon islands. Scientists Peter Pyle and Scot Anderson were recording great-white sharks attacking young elephant seals as they returned to the islands in the breeding season.

Leading wildlife film-maker Paul Atkins was dispatched to the Farallons to assess whether or not this could be filmed. He reported back that the potential was enormous but that

any operation would be time-consuming and involve a considerable amount of luck. Soon after his report other researchers in the Natural History Unit discovered another exciting area of great-white shark research, this time in South Africa. Here sharks were observed catching fur seal pups in a channel off Dyer island. The first ever film about natural great-white shark behaviour now looked feasible. We decided to seize the opportunity which had arisen by proposing a one hour 'Special' project to the controller who promptly endorsed the idea and the head of the unit, Alastair Fothergill, was awarded the commission. The hunt for the real 'Jaws' was on.

Paul Atkins and his wife Gracie took on the task. Paul realised that while he could film the sharks safely from the surface in a small boat, underwater footage would be more of a problem. Believe it or not, great-whites are timid creatures and to enter the water while they were feeding would almost certainly scare them off. If it did not the underwater cameraman would certainly find the experience frightening since these Farallon great-white sharks are some of the biggest in the world, up to 6 m (c. 20 ft) long with the girth of a mini-bus! To overcome this obstacle, Paul teamed up with one of the most experienced and inventive underwater cameramen in the wildlife filming business, Peter Scoones. Peter had developed a system of 'remote' underwater video cameras that

could be operated from a boat and so, for the first time, great-whites could be filmed going about their business undisturbed. After several months of work, bobbing around the cold Pacific waters that surround the Farallons, the Atkins and Peter, with the scientists' constant help, had obtained extraordinary pictures of magnificent sharks, attacking and feeding on elephant seals. They had also revealed social behaviour between the sharks, some of which was completely new to the scientists.

In South Africa the same camera team was joined by Doug Allan. While Peter concentrated on the underwater filming, Doug tried to film the moment of attack on a fur seal pup as the great-white, rushing from below the surface, actually shot out of the water with its prey in its jaws. To do this a platform was constructed in the hunting channel. Doug had to sit on it all day in the baking summer sun watching, through his telephoto lens, pups that had drifted away from the protection of main rafts of fur seals and become potential targets for the sharks. When an attack came it was with little warning and at a terrifying speed. As the 'slow motion' camera Doug was using took a couple of seconds to attain its running speed, he always had to anticipate the attack before it came. Eventually, after many days and many rolls of film, he succeeded.

Meanwhile Peter's remote cameras which, used off the side of a boat, had produced excellent results in California, were not working out so well in South Africa. The sharks and the fur seals would not behave naturally near to boats and so Peter came up with another plan. He had noticed that the sharks were often 'mobbed' by adult seals as they swam through certain sections of the channel. The seals were following the sharks in an attempt to ward off a surprise attack. However it was a dangerous strategy as sometimes the shark would turn on the seals and catch one. Peter thought he could film this behaviour by setting up cameras in the right location on the sea bed and subsequently operating them from the shore. Scuba diving into the 'hot spot' he attached his remote recording equipment to the sea floor and then negotiated an unmolested return to the shore . The system worked and he was able to capture the seal and shark drama from a safe haven on land.

Great White Shark, complete with a powerful introduction and narration by David Attenborough, was a filming triumph, ensuring us support for the present series in its wake. But what other subjects could live up to this legend of the deep and reveal themselves in such a new light? The first creature that sprang to mind was the wolf. There is a sad irony to this animal. Nearly all of us have touched a wolf or even kept one as a pet, for the domestic dog is now known to be genetically identical to the wolf. In its wild form, however, very few people have even glimpsed one, for it has become an outlaw right across its northern hemisphere range. Few animals have been subjected to as much persecution. Those that have survived in their natural habitat are, wisely, very wary of people, making the wild wolf one of the most difficult animals in the world to film. Indeed very few film sequences of wild wolves exist, the ones usually shown being of captive animals in large enclosures. Films about captive wolves may well show them in beautiful close-up but they reveal little about how wolves exist in the

wild. So a great challenge to the wildlife film-maker remained - a programme about wolves, shot only in their natural surroundings.

To take up this challenge you first need to find places where wild wolf packs just might tolerate people. Our researcher, Michelle Thompson, started the long hunt for any possibilities. She was helped by one of the Natural History Unit's most experienced producers, Mike Salisbury, whose previous productions like *Kingdom of the Ice Bear* had sent him on the trail of wolves before. For months no reliable locations came to light. The chances of spending too much time and money in the remotest parts of North America and then returning without results, looked ominously large. Mike and I decided to shelve the wolf challenge for now.

The situation changed when Canadian wildlife film-maker Jeff Turner visited the unit. Jeff had been having some remarkable success filming wolves for *The Natural World* in Canada's Wood Buffalo National Park and he thought this could be improved upon. By coincidence Michelle simultaneously discovered an apparently promising research project on wolves in Arctic Greenland. Other wolf studies in India and Romania also suggested potential for filming. It was beginning to look as though the delicate balance between success and failure had shifted slightly in our favour. Although

LOUIS GAGNON

Grey wolf.

Hugh Miles on location for
Kingdom of the Ice Bear,
waiting to film polar bear cubs at
Svalbard in March 1984.

we were frequently to regret it, Mike and I decided to go ahead with a 'Special' about the wild wolf.

Mike Salisbury also played a large part in starting a second potential Special on the polar bear. Ten years before, Mike and wildlife film-maker Hugh Miles had shot the now famous Arctic series *Kingdom of the Ice Bear*. The first programme had concentrated on the ice bear itself and few will ever forget some of the remarkable events shown within it. A highlight for me, and one of the greatest wildlife sequences I have ever seen, is that of the mother polar bear leaving her den for the first time, sliding down a snow bank, and then returning to her tiny cubs which were seeing daylight for the first time.

But despite achievements like this, both Mike and Hugh knew that the 'ultimate' polar bear film was still to be made. They had shown no more than a tantalising glimpse of the polar bear's life. Their achievements, great though they were, had been limited by the unique difficulties involved in filming polar bears, but they knew they now had the necessary techniques to probe the bear's life-cycle more deeply.

Among the various obstacles presented by polar bears is the fact that they are the largest carnivore on land and can be very dangerous. Next, since they live in the Arctic, the physical conditions are almost always harsh and often life-threatening. But the real problem is that they hunt on sea ice and the ice can break up with little warning. Being stranded on a disintegrating ice floe is about as bad as it gets in our business. All these problems can be overcome, with experience, but there is a final almost insurmountable one. Polar bears are not only scarce, but they range over thousands of kilometres of the Arctic's frozen waters, making it a rare event even to find a polar bear, let alone film one.

It was clear that Mike's experience could narrow the odds of failure with polar bears but then his own future plans changed. David Attenborough had proposed a new major series about birds and Mike Salisbury was the best person to lead its production. So we needed a new team for the polar

bear film, with the experience to overcome the unique hazards this programme presented. There was one obvious choice for cameraman, Doug Allan. Doug had started his career with the British Antarctic Survey and so was no stranger to the cold. As a cameraman, he had subsequently filmed many sequences in the Arctic, both above and below the ice, for series like *The Trials of Life* and had made a major contribution to the BBC's Antarctic series *Life in the Freezer*. Doug could certainly cope with the conditions and was skilled in the filming of polar bears. For some of the project he would link up with Martin Saunders, another cameraman with enormous experience who had taken on the polar bear challenge several times before. The producer is also a key person in any programme-making team as he or she must take ultimate responsibility for research and the safe organisation of filming, while keeping an editorial eye on the content and control over escalating costs. Martha Holmes took on this job. A marine biologist by training, she had originally joined the Natural History Unit as a presenter of underwater programmes such as *Sea Trek*, somehow managing to talk coherently in a diving 'bubble helmet' (which resembled an inverted goldfish bowl) as sharks gnawed at her or sea lions tugged at her communication cords. Martha is used to adventure. She was, having been

a member of the *Life in the Freezer* team, familiar with the dangers of the polar regions but she had yet to meet a polar bear. The team was good, but without luck their chances of filming the legendary ice bear were remote.

We wanted *The Wildlife Specials* to include a wide variety of animal types and decided that one film should be about a bird. Of all the birds, eagles are the most spectacular. In the past, films have concentrated on the habits of eagles when nesting and therefore confined to one place, but little has been shown of the rest of their lives. We needed a film that would travel with the eagle and reveal its aerial world. The best producer for this job was the creator of the classic natural history series *Supersense* and *Lifesense*, John Downer. He had already developed many extraordinary methods of enabling cameras to fly alongside birds when, in 1987, he made a film called *The In-flight Movie* for *Wildlife on One*. He continued to develop these techniques during *Supersense* and by the start of the Specials was still enhancing them, not by

Michael Richards films king penguin, watched by elephant seal, for Life in the Freezer.

Martha Holmes swimming with a whale shark off Hawaii in 1991 during filming of Sea Trek.

JOHN DOWNER

A remote camera was used for filming aerial shots during the making of Supersense.

JASON VENUS

Geoffrey Bell and remote control filming helicopter.

David Attenborough filming
for Private Life of Plants.

Michael Richards and king
penguin rookery during filming
of Life in the Freezer.

PETER BASSETT

now for television programmes, but for TV commercials and feature films. John had progressed considerably since his early days with the Natural History Unit but was enthusiastic about taking on a special film about eagles. He teamed up with Michael Richards, a renowned wildlife cameraman, especially when it comes to birds, who had worked with John throughout most of his career. The third member of the team was Neil Lucas, a director with extraordinary technical talents who can organise a film camera to fly down a street in New York, sit on a bird's back, or plunge into the ocean in a breathtaking dive. He is also a superb naturalist and a good companion when you are in a fix in the middle of a desert or remote jungle.

While the wolf, polar bear and eagle films were getting under way one of the most fruitful partnerships in wildlife filming, Owen Newman and Amanda Barrett, were completing a *Wildlife on One* film about leopards in Zambia's South Luangwa National Park. Owen and Amanda are masters when it comes to filming the big cats. Together they have made award-winning films about cheetahs, lions and leopards. While filming leopards, they had been experimenting with a special video camera which required very little light to record this largely nocturnal cat's activities. This had been a big step forward, as previous attempts to film leopards at night had involved using very bright filming lights which

dazzled either the leopard or its unfortunate prey. Nevertheless, what had been filmed in this way could hardly be described as 'natural behaviour'. Owen and Amanda completed their film *Night of the Leopard* but still felt that a big part of the leopard's story remained untold. They were convinced that nearly all of a leopard's hunting was undertaken after the moon had set, in pitch darkness. If this was so, then the most crucial period of a leopard's life was not being recorded, but Amanda and Owen knew what they had to do to check out their hunch - they had to develop a technique of filming with infra-red cameras and lights. Infra-red light is invisible to our eyes, and those of other mammals and birds, but if the night is illuminated with infra-red light an infra-red sensitive camera can obtain a picture as clear as one taken in daylight. Re-equipped, Owen and Amanda returned to Zambia in order to start work on a leopard Special and reveal its true night-time world.

In a selection of the world's most dramatic animals one cannot ignore giant reptiles such as the crocodile. This group of predators has survived largely unchanged since the time of the dinosaurs. There have been many excellent films about crocodiles but these have concentrated on just a few species and a limited amount of behaviour. Producer Karen Bass, who had made a number of award-winning

Martha Holmes and Mike de Gruy presenters of Sea Trek, feeding butterflyfish in Hawaii.

John Downer filming imprinted teal from a parascender for Supersense.

Richard Kirby filming in the western Australian desert for The Private Life of Plants.

programmes that looked in detail at animal groups, such as frogs, toads (*The Toad Skin Spell*) and primates (*Monkey in the Mirror*), took on the crocodiles. She began, with the assistance of researcher Gavin Maxwell, an exhaustive study to find out everything there was to know about crocodiles. This not only encompassed the scientific literature but also the experience of other film-makers who had watched crocodiles in the past. What became clear was that the only way to give a comprehensive view of crocodile behaviour was to film

them in many parts of the world, during the day and at night, on the surface and underwater. Karen was taking on an organisational nightmare and she would need a camera operator with an all encompassing knowledge of photographic techniques. Such a genius is Richard Kirby, a cameraman who has honed his skills on a wide range of exacting subjects, from microscopic algae to displaying birds of paradise. Richard has always taken on technically demanding films and was one of the mainstays of David Attenborough's last major series *The Private Life of Plants*, filming exquisite time-lapse sequences which have changed our view of plants for ever. He is also a meticulous field

Killer whale attacking a sea lion
on the shores of the Valdez
peninsula, Argentina.

naturalist and recently demonstrated his talents as one of the two cameramen filming previously unrecorded displays of birds of paradise in the remotest parts of New Guinea for one of David's most remarkable programmes, *Attenborough in Paradise*. One way or another the combination of Karen Bass and Richard Kirby was certain to result in a very different crocodile film.

The giant marine mammals are also prime candidates for a series like this. Initially we decided to research the possibility of a film about the killer whale. Australian wildlife film-makers, David and Elizabeth Parer, had recently completed a remarkable killer whale film. Anything we did would have to surpass that great achievement. As the killer whale research came in, each potential location revealed major obstacles. It was obvious that if we proceeded, this film could turn into a total disaster. As we gloomily pondered our killer whale prospects, American wildlife cameraman Rick Rosenthal came up with another idea. Rick, a specialist in filming marine mammals, was completing a film on the sperm whale . The next whale he had in his sights was the humpback. The general perception of the humpback whale, and one which I am sad to say I shared, was of a slow-moving, plankton-sieving leviathan, hardly a match for the dynamic killer whale. Rick soon re-educated me to realise that the humpback is possibly the most sophisticated

fish-eating predator in the ocean and, though difficult to film, a perfect candidate for the series. Rick teamed up with Andy Byatt, a Natural History Unit producer with a love of the sea and considerable experience working above and below it and together they started their Special.

These were the teams that set out in 1996 on their very different challenges and their extraordinary experiences provide a fascinating insight into the vicissitudes of tracking and filming animals in the wild.

Polar bear

MARTHA HOLMES

Polar bears are so well adapted to the cold that they can happily sleep in the worst Arctic storms at subzero temperatures.

JEFF FOOTT

Polar bears may travel thousands of miles in search of food.

POLAR BEARS are the largest land carnivores on Earth. They also have the reputation of being the most dangerous. But, looking back on our months of polar living, it was not only working with bears that exhilarated and tested us, it was the Arctic itself: the bitter cold, cruel winds and, as it turned out, the unpredictable nature of the ice. Despite the demands of living in an often inhospitable place, it was usually the bears which caused the greatest difficulties. They did not threaten us or attack us, but simply remained frustratingly elusive.

The Arctic is a big place. Lacking the land mass of Antarctica, it is formed instead by a vast frozen sea flanked by scattered archipelagos, a few large islands including Greenland, and by the continents of America and Eurasia. Although polar bears are found throughout the Arctic, and are known to cover great distances on foot, they seem to be segregated into geographically discrete populations. Bears living in Canada's Hudson Bay, for example, probably do not mix with those living on the north coast of Alaska.

Given that there are so called 'good' polar bear areas, one might be forgiven for thinking that finding them to film would be a relatively straightforward task. But time and time again we had difficulty in locating bears so that days and weeks would go by without so much as a footprint in the snow.

Doug Allan in his snow hide with his specially winterised camera gear.

On our first trip to Svalbard, a group of islands north of Norway, cameraman Doug Allan and two Norwegian field assistants set off in search of female bears breaking out of their winter dens with young cubs. It was early March and still very cold; the Arctic was only just emerging from winter. Day after day, week after week, they scanned the hillsides along a 250 km (*c.* 150 mls) stretch of remote coastline in a race against time before the bears left their dens for the sea ice. Despite the fact that it was a known denning area, after six weeks of intensive exploration the exhausted team returned with hundreds of feet of film showing magnificent scenery, but not one inch depicting a polar bear mother with her cubs. For one brief period of the trip it seemed that the team's luck had changed. Having located a den, Doug built a snow hide some distance downwind in order to conceal his presence. He set up his camera equipment and waited patiently for the bears to emerge. After a few days of constant vigil a female bear did emerge - only to reveal a large radio collar around her neck.

The Arctic is remote and given the great distances we needed to cover through uninhabited territory, logistics became an enormous part of the operation. In addition to the camera gear, a mountain of boxes in its own right, we carried a huge quantity of equipment which was essential for our safety and survival. In spring we travelled by snow scooters, towing sledges stacked high with all our necessary provisions. A ten hour snow scooter trip in temperatures below -25°C is exciting for the first five minutes and then it is just a very long way. Our route took us over glaciers, mountains and frozen fjords and so the tedium of driving a noisy machine was alleviated by the majestic beauty of this land, empty of humanity. Our destination was a series of fjords in northern Svalbard in which there was every chance of seeing ringed seals and, with luck, a polar bear or two on the prowl. Whilst the scooters did enable us to cover huge distances, and to explore remote areas, they also consumed considerable quantities of fuel. In anticipation of this trip we had already made a fuel depot in the fjord the previous summer, a drop-off by kind courtesy of a tourist ship. In the event this proved inadequate and two refuelling expeditions all the way back to civilisation had to be mounted to keep us operating.

Whilst the extreme cold provided excellent snow and sea ice conditions for the scooters it was potentially dangerous for us humans. Layer upon layer of wool and fleece garments with not a millimetre of skin exposed anywhere were essential protection against frostbite. Two windproof balaclavas and a leather (the most windproof material of all) flying hat on top almost smothered us, but we still needed goggles and a mask to protect our faces. It invariably took some time to get dressed each day.

Martha Holmes and Martin Saunders at home in Texas Bar.

MATS FORSBERG

Our temporary home in northern Svalbard was a tiny hut, inexplicably named 'Texas Bar'. We arrived at midnight to find the hut largely buried under the snow and so had the immediate task of digging it out. What Texas Bar lacked in space and modern comforts, it made up for in its character and remote setting. A mere 2 m x 2.5 m (*ca.* 7 ft x 8 ft) of floor space contained a bunk, a table, a bench and a free standing wood burning stove. Into this tiny space we had to squeeze our party of three as well as all our camera and personal gear. Simple tasks, like going to bed, required logistical planning and good humour and we were even obliged to establish a strict order for getting ready and into our makeshift bunks. Suffocating from the heat of the stove as

Candles keep the only window in Texas Bar ice free.

MATS FORSBERG

THOMAS D. MANGELSEN

An 18 month old cub is still very dependent on its mother.

we went to sleep, we awoke bitterly cold with the fire long since dead. Often it was an inquisitive polar bear, breathing heavily against the diminutive window, or setting off the trip wire alarm which woke us.

We always took the potential danger posed by bears seriously. At this time of year, after a winter of little or no food, polar bears are hungry and so a hut containing food and three humans is more than enough to excite their curiosity. We surrounded Texas Bar with a trip wire and explosive flares which ignited when a bear approached too close, or when one of our party forgot to avoid the wire. But when we were away from the hut we had to use other strategies. The first line of defence towards an overly-interested bear was to act dominant, and the second was to use a flare gun which we carried with us at all times. As a last resort we had a rifle and a hand gun for the bears, but we assumed, rightly, that they would never have to be used. Few people travel in polar bear country without a rifle.

Whilst the polar bear's reputation for unprovoked attacks on people may not be entirely justified, those who know the animals well treat them with respect and appropriate caution. Such attacks, when they do occur, are usually by young bears that have left their mothers but are not yet good at hunting, or by old bears that have lost their hunting skills. Nevertheless most bears are extremely inquisitive and one that comes close will, understandably, cause concern, regardless of whether or not it means business. When in the Arctic it is well to remember that for much of the year polar bears of all ages are hungry and are on the look out for food.

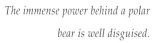

The immense power behind a polar

bear is well disguised.

MATS FORSBERG

Martin Saunders, a veteran of Arctic filming, was assigned the task of filming polar bears hunting. In late March, when ringed seals give birth to their pups, bears begin to concentrate in the fjords. Born in lairs under the snow, the vulnerable pups remain protected from the extreme cold and concealed from sight. But bears have a remarkably keen sense of smell and can easily detect a seal's hidden lair. Approaching stealthily, the bear positions itself at the edge of the lair and gradually rises up to stand on its hind legs. Suddenly, it crashes down onto the snow with its front legs, breaking through the roof to try and catch the seal or its pup before they escape into the sea beneath the ice. Martin managed to follow bears and film their dramatic hunting pounces a number of times. But polar bears are not always successful, indeed their success rate in hunting seals is less than 5 per cent, and we began to believe that cameraman-tolerant bears were even less efficient at catching seals than most. Sometimes they became more interested in Martin than the seals.

Another of our filming trips took us to Admiralty Inlet in Canada where it was not the bears which caused a problem, it was the very ice beneath our feet. We were there at the end of May, when the sun never sets, and once again we were hoping to film bears hunting as well as the return of migrant birds and whales. Admiralty Inlet opens onto Lancaster Sound and we were camped there, on the edge of the ice.

Ringed seals rest out on the ice but never far from their means of escape.

The white coat of the ringed seal pup acts as thermal protection and camouflage.

Polar bears are inquisitive and often stand to get a better view.

THOMAS D. MANGELSEN

We were a team of three: Doug Allan, myself and an Inuit guide called Shooyook. For ten days or so we had experienced variable weather and the worst of the storms had us building a snow wall for protection, retreating into one tent and securing that down with all our gear and giant blocks of snow. During a brief respite we saw the one and only bear of the trip at a great distance and also watched an ice-breaking ship make its slow but inexorable way south into Admiralty Inlet.

Shooyook, our Inuit guide, radios for help.

MARTHA HOLMES

Two days later, with a strong wind blowing from the south, we ventured forth late in the day to find the ice edge cleared of loose pack ice and dark water stretching as far as the eye could see. We were thrilled for this meant the beluga whales might now move in. The light was beautiful and Doug started filming fulmars flying over the ice edge. Shooyook had crossed the crack left by the ice-breaker to search for bears further along the ice edge. It seemed our fortunes had changed, but it was not long before our optimism evaporated.

I suddenly caught sight of Shooyook as he raced back towards us, unable to cross the crack which had now widened. He doubled back to the south and had to go a long way before he found a place to take his scooter across. As soon as he had negotiated the gap he sped towards us waving and shouting. I had never seen him so animated and it was clear that something was seriously wrong. Despite his broken English we soon understood his concern; the ice-breaker had destabilised the ice and strong winds had dislodged the sheet on which we were camped - we were adrift, and heading for the open sea.

Our 'Mayday' message was relayed, via various communities, to Resolute where the rescue plane was based, but they were experiencing a major storm and take-off was impossible. We could do absolutely nothing but wait. Huddled together in a makeshift shelter, it was only conversation and endless cups of tea which kept our worst fears at bay. The floe was by now far out into Lancaster Sound, and we were well aware that the battering by waves and strong currents was

We managed to fit everything but one snow scooter and the largest sledge into our rescue plane.

taking its toll on the thin slab of ice. After 20 hours of uncertainty we were relieved to hear on our radio that the storm over Resolute had cleared and the plane was on its way. We constructed a makeshift windsock out of a tarpaulin and guided the pilot to our floe by radio. Soon we were on board with most of our gear heading back to the community of Arctic Bay. The plane had to make a second trip to pick up the remaining snow scooter and found the ice floe had already split in two. It was a stern reminder of the unpredictable nature of the ice and the dangers involved in entering the polar bears' world. We were lucky. Despite all our equipment and combined experience we depended upon outside help for our rescue. Without radio contact and the timely clearing in the weather things might have turned out rather differently.

The arrival of summer transforms the Arctic; the ice retreats and the weather is kinder bringing forth battalions of mosquitoes. In some places, as the ice melts back polar bears are obliged to swim for shore, and we returned to Canada hoping to film bears in the water. After considerable research, the northern reaches of Hudson Bay seemed to offer the best opportunity. In fact, there were supposed to be so many bears in the area that people tried to discourage us from camping

Polar bears are often obliged to swim between melting ice floes.

in the area at all. But having just had a succession of almost bearless trips, it seemed like the right place to go and we had no option but to camp. We had momentary doubts when the pilot of the plane we chartered insisted on taking off as soon as possible, before any marauding bears appeared on the horizon. We set up the tents and awaited our guides who arrived by boat, just hours later, beaching on the gravel shoreline which had earlier served as our landing strip.

Ten days later, and half way through our planned stay, we still had not seen any bears and were becoming somewhat dispirited. During one of the nightly radio sessions that form part of life in this remote region, we heard of a polar bear some 200 km away. It was one more bear than we had seen so we decided to strike camp and move, by boat, in that direction. It was a turning point in the trip. En route to the new site we encountered a swimming bear - the first of many that we were able to film, both on ice floes and in the water.

During this entire trip we had not seen a bear on land, and consequently the trip-wire alarm system had not been erected around the tents - there seemed no need. Indeed my concern about bears in camp was not taken very seriously even though I was asked to take a flare gun with me when I went to wash. I was happy to do what they recommended; it seemed wise to respect the experience of men who had grown up in such a place.

MARTHA HOLMES

The guides insisted that, if they were going to help us on location, they be allowed to live off the land as they normally would, which meant killing seals and caribou. And so on our way back to the original landing beach, towards the end of this trip, one of the guides shot a seal for supper. That night I was woken by something on the gravel outside my tent; it was too close for comfort. I heard an animal breathing and I knew it was a bear. Alarmed, my heart hammering, I gradually opened my tent zip, tooth by tooth. Right in front of me sat a little polar bear cub, gazing up with surprise. Far from being

We found one large adult bear that accepted the close presence of our boat.

MARTHA HOLMES

*Doug Allan and his Inuit
guide were left on a drifting ice
floe to film steady shots of
swimming bears.*

*Polar bears easily overheat in
summer; swimming in such cold
water cools them down.*

MARTHA HOLMES

Ursus maritimus - *the sea bear.*

Our camp on the ice of Admiralty Inlet.

Cubs will typically stay with their mothers for two and a half years.

enchanted, I knew this had serious implications; the young cub's presence meant that a very protective mother would be nearby, but I had no idea where. Very, very slowly I eased my head out and looked around. Another cub was playing with our plates and behind the guides' tent was their mother. I decided to risk calling out, as loudly as I dared, 'Guys, we've got bears in camp.' At that the mother bear looked up, 'chuffed' and ran off, her cubs in tow. In order to scare her off, we emerged from our tents and made a great deal of noise before retiring again.

Seal blood, which had brought the bears into our camp in the first place, is an irresistible attraction to polar bears, and so it proved this night. Three hours later I woke to the sound of an angry growl, a tent ripping and then a shot. The bears had returned. The large female bear, having entangled herself in a guy rope, had growled and slashed out at the tent. The noise had woken our guides who, always lying with a rifle at hand, had fired a warning shot. Thankfully neither the bear nor any of us were injured. The following night we were on watch.

Probably the most difficult polar bear sequence to film is the birth of cubs in a snow den. I consulted numerous polar bear scientists about this and they were unanimous in their opinion - it could not be done. The female bear, we were warned, would desert her den if she was disturbed as she was settling down in the autumn and even if this hurdle was overcome she would certainly investigate and destroy any strange objects hidden in the wall of her den. Clearly, trying to achieve this in the wild was a hopeless task, even with the newest technology and the tiniest cameras.

Polar bear cubs are born minute, weighing only 0.5 kg (1 lb); their mothers are about 1000 times heavier, a quite astonishing difference. A sequence of a female bear and her newly born cub together seemed an important element of the polar bear story we were trying to tell. We contacted every zoo in the world that had breeding polar bears and eventually opted for one in Belgium. There was a large element of risk in this plan because even a vet cannot confirm if a polar bear is pregnant. Our chosen bear had mated in spring and her keeper had a hunch that she was pregnant, but that was all

Females with cubs are always wary and give other bears a wide berth.

A polar bear mother protects her cub on an ice floe.

we had to go on. Plans for the maternity den were drawn up and building began. We wanted to film the birth using infra-red lights so that the bear could remain in darkness. Three remote infra-red cameras were put in position on pan-and-tilt heads so that the whole den could be filmed. Our major concern at this point was that we were running out of time and the bear needed to become accustomed to the den before she was confined.

Then we had a whole catalogue of disasters, some more serious than others. The glass that had to be specially made to a safe thickness turned out to be infra-red absorbing; we had to use low level white light instead. The bear, on her first night in the den, banged on the exit door which was coated with a red rust-proof paint, long since dry but powdery. She proceeded to cover herself and the white den in red dust. Luckily it rained the next day so she was brought out to have a shower and clean herself off. When she returned to the repainted den, much to our delight, she accepted it. A few days later the cameras rolled as she gave birth to two tiny cubs.

When you film polar bears in their own habitat you enter a totally different world. The Arctic can be a savagely cold wilderness that throws impossible challenges at you without warning, but it is a place that has many moods and there are times when it is an exquisitely lit, serene white wilderness. Polar bears are equally changeable. Their physical power inspires awe and commands respect and yet they can bewitch you with their charm. To have worked with so magnificent an animal in such a place has been an extraordinary privilege.

MATS FORSBERG

In Hudson Bay polar bears are stranded on land during summer. As the cool of autumn returns and they await freeze-up, male bears 'play' fight to hone their technique and assess their rank before the real fights take place over females and food.

THOMAS D MANGELSEN

THOMAS D MANGELSEN

THOMAS D MANGELSEN

Polar bear

Ursus maritimus

JEFF FOOTT

MATS FORSBERG

GENERAL DESCRIPTION

Polar bears, which may be more than 3 m (9 ft 9 ins) tall when standing on their hind legs, are large heavily built mammals with rough coats. Their fur varies from white in winter to creamy yellow in summer and their skin is black. Males, weighing 350-650 kgs (*c.* 770-1430 lbs) (record 800 kgs/1760 lbs), have a much heavier build than females which weigh 150-500 kgs (*c.* 330-1100 lbs). The male's face is often scarred by fights. As they age the fur on the muzzle thins out to reveal black skin beneath. Older male bears often have broken canines. They may 'chuff' when anxious while females utter a low-pitched 'bawl', not unlike a sea lion, and cubs can respond with a similar but higher pitched 'maaaw-maaaw' sound.

Polar bears have a circumpolar distribution, though at generally very low population densities, and there are several geographically distinct populations.

BREEDING AND REARING OF YOUNG

The breeding season is from early March to late June. There are still gaps in our knowledge of their natural mating behaviour. What we do know is that mating takes place on sea ice. The male may remain with the female for over two weeks, mating often. There may be more than one male trailing the female but only one has access to her. Interaction involves gentle rolling, pawing, sliding and face to face contact. After fertilisation, eggs do not become implanted in the wall of the uterus for three to four months, until September or October. After a very short gestation period of 60 days the mother gives birth, typically to two, but sometimes to one or three cubs, in a snow den constructed either on land or on the sea ice, depending on the region. At birth the cubs are 30 cm (*c.* 1 ft) long, and weigh 0.5 kg (*c.* 1 lb). We know little of their behaviour while still in the den but once they emerge they are playful and inquisitive, learning by imitation of their mother. They remain under parental protection for usually two and a half years, but occasionally as long as three and a half, or in the case of cubs observed at Churchill, for as little as one and a half years. By the time they emerge from the den the cubs weigh approximately 10 kgs (c. 22 lbs) and thereafter their growth depends greatly on the hunting success of the mother (hence the great variation in how long cubs stay with their mother).

MOVEMENT AND FEEDING

THOMAS D. MANGELSEN

Polar bears living in different areas display varying patterns of seasonal movement, influenced by ice conditions. In southern populations, such as at Hudson Bay, the ice melts totally and the bears are obliged to spend all summer and autumn on land. Elsewhere they remain on the retreating ice.

Their preferred food is ringed seals, (and sometimes bearded seals) but in the absence of these species, will eat almost anything including beluga, reindeer, walrus, narwhal, birds' eggs, carrion, kelp, moss, and berries. During springtime they pound their way through seal pup lairs underneath the snow. The most important hunting period is from April to July. Hunting in mid-summer involves a polar bear sitting and lying for hour after hour by a seal's breathing hole and then catching it with paw and mouth as it comes up for air. They also engage in 'aquatic stalking': hunting seals that are basking on ice by approaching their prey along melt channels, thus keeping a low profile until the moment of attack. In autumn they are reduced to scavenging and eating vegetation such as berries. In Wrangel Island they will attack walruses by rushing at the herd and homing in on the pups. In winter they hunt ringed seals on sea ice, but with reduced success.

RESEARCH

There is still a lot to learn about polar bears but research in the Arctic is costly and scientific expeditions are constrained, both by the environment and by budgetary considerations. Studies have been undertaken into potentially sustainable levels of hunting polar bears with a view to regulating how many bears can be killed. Other research has looked at the physiology of bears to see how they cope with the prolonged starvation periods that they are forced to endure.

The difficulties of counting an animal dispersed at low densities over vast areas are considerable and involve significant investments in terms of personnel, equipment and funds. Estimated population sizes for Canada, Alaska and west Greenland are probably not too far off the mark but counts for the rest of their range, including Russia, are problematic.

With the exception of data from Wrangel and Herald, together with some information from Franz Joseph Land, we still do not know the extent of denning areas in Russia.

Scientists are beginning to gain some understanding of the relationship between bears, seals, ice conditions and fluctuations that occur with varying ecological conditions and longer term climate change.

Present research on polar bears is focusing on refining estimates of population size, defining population boundaries through satellite tracking of animals fitted with radio collars, studying ecological relationships of polar bears and seals, monitoring for possible long-term effects of contaminants, and investigation of metabolic pathways for recycling fats.

These studies have revealed the following new information on polar bears:
- Radio tracking reveals major differences between the behaviour of individual bears. Whereas some may remain within relatively small areas of around 100 kms by 200 kms (c. 60 x 120 mls), others may wander over an area exceeding 250,000 sq. kms. in a single year.
- Polar bears can turn on or off a low-energy consuming state of hibernation, as their needs dictate. This contrasts sharply with the black bear which can only do so on a seasonal basis. This facility is a vital adaptation for polar bears since it allows them to regulate their activities depending on the availability of food.

Although we tend to think of bears as efficient killing machines, in good areas the average kill rate is often no more than one seal every five or more days and for some bears it is much lower. The ability to scavenge and to adjust its metabolic rate form important elements in the bears' overall survival.

CONSERVATION

The population is thought to be relatively stable at present, at around 20,000 to 30,000 individuals. However, any factor that increases mortality of adult females can have a dramatic impact. If 2 per cent of adult females are harvested, the population will decline. Any warming, or cooling, of the Arctic, or any other change in the weather or ice conditions could be catastrophic as it would also affect the ringed seal population on which bears depend for their staple food.

The extent of poaching on polar bears in Russia is unknown, as are the effects of contaminant accumulation due to pollution of the Arctic marine ecosystem.

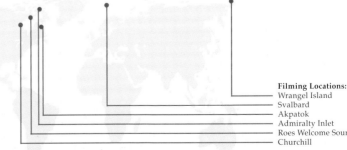

Filming Locations:
Wrangel Island
Svalbard
Akpatok
Admiralty Inlet
Roes Welcome Sound
Churchill

W o l f

MIKE SALISBURY

Two piercing amber eyes looked unfalteringly into mine.

Wildlife cameraman Jeff Turner in the brushwood hide.

A PALE SHADOW briefly appears between the dark trunks of the fir trees and then disappears again. Was it a wolf? Or, in the first glimmer of daylight, merely a trick of the imagination? If it does come closer it will be my first glimpse of a wolf in the wild. The pulse quickens. Next to me, crouching in our rough brushwood hide, is Dr Lu Carbyn, one of the world's foremost wolf biologists. He signals complete silence and then gives a 'maybe - maybe not' sign to wildlife cameraman Jeff Turner, who is also poised by his camera in anticipation.

We had crawled quietly into the hide, armed with thick sleeping bags, two hours before daybreak when a heavy layer of hoar frost covered the vegetation. The three holes in the front wall gave each of us a good view across the narrow creek where, 25 m (55 ft) away, the bloated carcass of a buffalo that must have fallen through the ice sometime during the winter, lay stranded on the far bank. We knew wolves had already fed on it from the numerous footprints in the mud; now we wanted to capture the occasion on film.

The light increases and Jeff looks happier - at least now he's registering an exposure reading. A raven cronks, breaking the spell of silence and, as if on cue, a very large white wolf suddenly materialises on the crest of the opposite bank. As the magnificent animal moves cautiously down the steep slope to the water's edge, I listen to the reassuring whir of film running through Jeff's camera. Just before drinking from the river, the wolf stares in our direction and, through my binoculars, two piercing amber eyes look unfalteringly into mine. It is one of those mesmerizing moments when contact with an animal seems to surpass a mere observation and touch on something more fundamental. Later I wonder if this is the sort of experience that has polarised human attitudes over the centuries, into either wonder and respect of wolves or fear of them as evil adversaries.

MIKE SALISBURY

JOSE SCHELL

Grey wolf feeding at a kill.

For eight days we crept in and out of this hide as Jeff gradually built up a useful film sequence. On one memorable occasion, two wolves swam across the mirror-calm creek, distorting the reflections of the surrounding forest. On another day, a brown bear with her two cubs came to feed on the carcass and chased off an approaching wolf who disappeared into the trees with its tail between its legs. Some days, our long vigils went unrewarded; neither wolf nor bear appeared and no film passed through the camera. We knew that our sustained efforts might provide, if we were lucky, no more than a two or three minute sequence, but such is the nature of wildlife filming, especially when one's subjects are as elusive and enigmatic as wolves.

Wood Buffalo National Park, where we were based for this filming, is a vast wilderness area in the Canadian State of Northern Alberta. Dr Lu Carbyn has been going there regularly for the last 15 years or more and, through immensely patient field work, has acquired an unrivalled knowledge of the Western timber wolves that inhabit the area. These have the distinction of being the only wolves in the world that still prey on buffalo as their main source of food. Over the years, Lu has followed the migrating herds of buffalo to their favoured grazing areas and has often witnessed the remarkable spectacle of a large pack of wolves chasing and

These wolves, with their highly-tuned senses, are fully aware of our presence; our hide hasn't fooled them, but they choose on this occasion to ignore us. Jeff films as two of the bolder ones feed on the carcass and then drink again from the river. A distant howl alerts them and they both throw up their heads and howl back. Others join in from where they have been hidden in the trees and now the forest echoes with their eerie calls. When the howling stops the wolves melt back into the trees as silently as they had arrived.

Delivery by boat . . . after that, foot travel only was allowed.

A herd of buffalo cross one of the tree-lined creeks.

pulling down one of these huge prey animals. He also knew some of the wolves' den sites and their rendezvous areas where, in late summer and autumn, the pups are left guarded by one or two adults while the rest go out hunting. Lu generously offered to share this hard-won knowledge with Canadian wildlife film-makers Jeff and Sue Turner for this Wildlife Special about wolves.

The wilderness area where the wolves and buffalo live is about the size of Denmark, and consists mainly of a huge inland delta formed by the Peace and Athabasca Rivers where they empty into Athabasca Lake. Much of the terrain consists of marshy grassland, interlaced by lakes and creeks of varying sizes, whose raised banks are often lined by thick forests of fir and aspen. No motorised transport of any sort is allowed

A helicopter delivers the canoes.

Wolf biologist, Dr Lu Carbyn,
(nearest the camera) and an
assistant try easing
the load with
a two-wheeled cart.

for travelling within the Park so once everything has been delivered by boat or helicopter, the only way to get around is on foot, or by canoe. I soon learnt what an exhausting business it was to move from camp to camp, or try to keep pace with a pack of wolves, on foot, while carrying all the camera gear in rucksacks!

In the course of his research into wolf behaviour, Lu Carbyn had already discovered that it was best to keep pace with the buffalo herds in the hope that, once they settled to graze, a

pack of wolves might creep up and attempt a kill. Jeff adopted a similar method, which proved especially difficult, since the particular herd that he chose to follow seemed to be in a constant state of alert, even whilst steadily feeding. Approaching close enough for filming involved tip-toeing under cover of the bushes or crawling very slowly through the long, soaking wet grass. As soon as one's presence was revealed a buffalo would invariably snort in alarm and the whole herd would start to run. Once buffalo are on the move

JEFF & SUE TURNER

A vast wilderness area the size of Denmark. The delta grasslands in mid-summer.

they often travel 5 or 10 km before pausing to graze again. For the film crew each such disturbance meant that the stealthy and laborious process of getting to within camera range of the herd had to begin all over again!

Camping out in such a wilderness helped me to appreciate the kind of conditions wolves will always need if they are to survive the human persecution which they have attracted for so long. To be woken up in a tent, at three in the morning, by a pack of wolves howling in full voice about a hundred metres away, is an unforgettable experience. So too, is travelling at night across this seemingly endless grassland while the brilliant *aurora borealis* provides pulsating curtains of coloured lights overhead. Or to wake on a sharply frosty

dawn to the sight and sound of wave upon wave of snow geese and whooper swans heading north on their spring migration. Or to canoe silently down a glassy creek where only water fowl, the occasional musk rat or beaver breaks the reflection of the ancient forest lining each bank. Or to follow the unmistakable paw prints of a wolf along a muddy buffalo trail through the old-growth forest knowing that you might be the first human being ever to have passed that way. Then in a clearing to surprise a very large adult male wolf drinking from a puddle at only 20 paces distant, make a few seconds eye-contact, and then watch in awe as he calmly turns his back to trot unhurriedly across the open space before silently disappearing, like a pale ghost, into the trees beyond.

*To be woken up by wolves
howling a hundred metres away
is an unforgettable experience.*

MIKE SALISBURY

Jeff Turner on the look-out
for wolves.

JEFF & SUE TURNER

In his own more prolonged visits to Wood Buffalo National Park, Jeff Turner, through incredible patience and physical effort was eventually able to film more aspects of wild timber wolf behaviour than has ever been achieved. In midwinter, with the temperature dipping to -30°C, he recorded how a pack of 20 wolves harassed a small herd of buffalo in the snow for seven whole days and nights before making a kill. In spring, he filmed how the wolves tried to separate a small buffalo calf away from its mother, and how the mother bravely chased the attackers off. In late summer, he filmed a new litter of wolf pups venturing away from their maternity den for the first time, and then being fed at a rendezvous site by the returning adults who regurgitated some of the half-digested meat from their stomachs. And in the burnished colours of autumn he managed to gain the trust of a partic-ularly large pack of wolves, with their pups now fully grown, to film them all howling in full orchestral splendour, before setting off on a hunt.

The hope, when making a programme about as enigmatic an animal as the wolf, is that eventually, given time and persistence, you will be in the right place at the right time to film some nugget of behaviour that will be memorable for years to come. That chance came to Jeff early one spring morning when Lu Carbyn reported seeing a nearby herd of buffalo milling around in a disturbed manner. Jeff, Lu and Anton Pauw, his field assistant for this trip, grabbed the tripod lenses and camera and ran about half a mile towards

Immature grey wolf.

A fully grown bull buffalo can weigh more than a ton.

the scene. Sweating profusely, they were just in time for Jeff to set up the camera and start filming as the entire herd of buffalo thundered towards them at full speed. Snapping at the buffaloes' heels in hot pursuit were a pack of wolves trying to get at the calves which were being sheltered in the middle of the herd of running adults. As the chase developed around him, the scene that Jeff recorded on film was immediately destined to become a classic sequence. Not only was it unique action footage, but it evoked to stunning effect the scenes that must have taken place every day on the great grassland plains of North America a century earlier, before wolves were mercilessly eradicated by the advancing hordes of European cattle ranchers.

Soon after this, Jeff also managed to film a pack of wolves pulling down an adult buffalo, which, after putting up a long defence and trying to escape into the river, was eventually killed and eaten by the wolves. This again was behaviour which had hardly ever been witnessed by biologists, let alone filmed.

Wolf tracks in the mud.
The feet are much wider than
those of a fox or coyote.

Patterns in the snow depict a
wolf pack's long struggle to
bring down a buffalo.

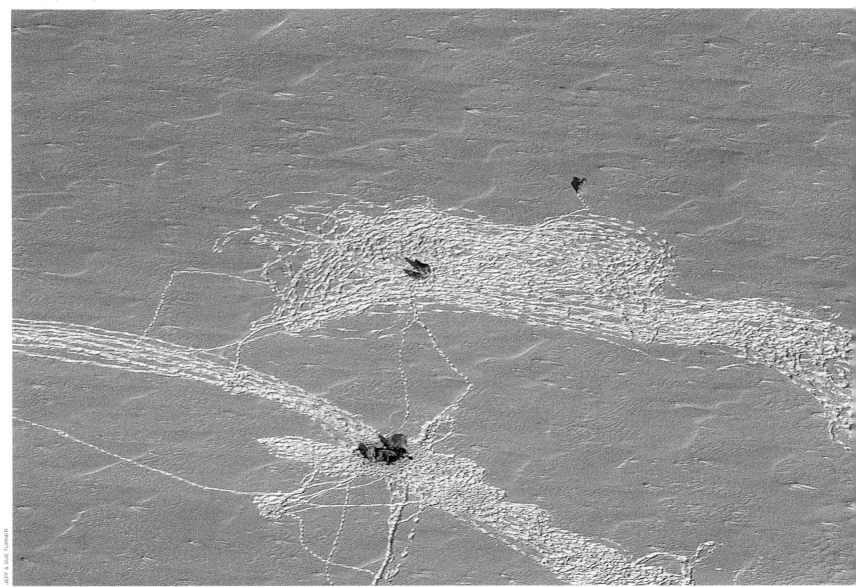

An Indian wolf on the hunt . . .

in the background are the

blackbuck it will try to catch.

Meanwhile, thousands of miles from Canada, wildlife cameraman Ian McCarthy, with his field assistant Tom Clarke, were becoming acquainted with some wolves living in a very different environment. Based in the State of Maharashtra, their aim was to film the increasingly endangered Indian wolf, the most southerly living of all the world's remaining wolves. They were being studied here by Dr Satish Kumar who was to help the film team with his knowledge of their habits, built up over several years of patient research.

Smaller than timber wolves, Indian wolves also have thinner, sleeker coats and could initially be mistaken for oversized jackals; but their long legs and large paws leave no doubting their identity as true wolves. Unlike the wilderness of Northern Alberta where any human disturbance is minimal, the area in which these Indian wolves were living was a relatively small reserve surrounded by burgeoning farming activity, much of which involved the herding of domestic animals. When he started filming, Ian immediately noticed that he could often hear the sound of Indian music or human voices in the distance, and Satish Kumar soon confirmed that the wolves quite often took sheep and goats, an activity which was naturally making them very unpopular with the local herdsmen. However, it was now the monsoon period, with considerable numbers of blackbuck migrating into the reserve to take advantage of the fresh grazing, so the wolves had less need to prey on domestic stock.

It took Ian and Tom several days to 'tune in' to the wolves' behaviour. To have any chance of filming a worthwhile sequence they needed to learn, for instance, the various places where the parents left their three pups when they went out hunting. When the adults did set off for a hunt, Ian needed to locate a suitable vantage point from which he could film the action. With the patience and dedication that forms an essential requirement for all top wildlife camera people, Ian eventually succeeded in filming an excellent sequence of pup behaviour and an exciting blackbuck chase involving the entire pack. The latter is a game in which the blackbuck usually come off best and, viewing Ian's slow-motion footage of the way these wonderfully agile antelopes, while running at full speed, bounce or 'pronk' 2 m (c. 6 ft 6 ins) or so into the air to confuse their predators, the lack of hunting success doesn't seem so strange. But the wolves' poor showing against this wild game spells even greater pressure on their survival since the more they turn to easier prey, such as goats or sheep, the more understandably intolerant local farmers become of their activities.

Grey wolves on the lookout

for white-tailed deer.

DAVID WELLING

The warning snarl of a wolf . . . of little danger to man but the sort of image that gave the wolf a bad name.

At a deer kill, the dominant male's snarl reminds the other members of the pack exactly who is boss!

JEFF FOOTT

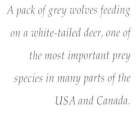

A pack of grey wolves feeding on a white-tailed deer, one of the most important prey species in many parts of the USA and Canada.

The chequered relationship that has existed over the centuries between man and wolf formed a vital part of our story. Assistant Producer, Michelle Thompson, apart from researching all the scientific aspects of wolf biology, and where best to film them in the wild, had also unearthed many fascinating stories to illustrate both the latest methods of researching wolf behaviour and the ways in which attitudes to wolves may at last be changing. Documenting these aspects took Michelle, cameraman Ian McCarthy, sound recordist Trevor Gosling, and production co-ordinator Anne Holmes to a variety of locations mainly in the USA and Canada. In northern Minnesota they filmed Dr Dave Mech (one of the world's foremost wolf biologists) and his colleague Dr Mike Nelson carrying out aerial radio tracking surveys as part of a long-term study of wolf movements and territory sizes. In Idaho they filmed a heart-warming interview with Horace, one of the elders of the Nez Perce tribe, as he vividly described how he looked into the eyes and personally welcomed the first of several wolves to be released onto Nez Perce tribal lands in the hope of re-establishing a population of these much admired predators, after an absence of nearly 100 years. In Montana they visited the Nine Mile Valley in order to film the wild wolves migrating there, of their own volition, from Canada. Their story tells how a pair of wolves travelled through 150 miles of hostile ranching country to arrive, as if guided by wolf intuition, at the one ranch in the valley where they could be guaranteed a warm welcome and where they soon produced their first litter of pups. Today, after a few initial setbacks, a growing wolf population is gradually gaining human acceptance in Montana, a state where only 30 years or so ago they would have been wiped off the face of the earth as unwanted vermin.

The team also wanted to shoot an optimistic sequence for the end of the film, one that would illustrate the recent improvement in people's attitudes towards wolves. To this end we attended a 'wolf howl' in Algonquin National Park in southern Canada where, on four or five August nights each year, park authorities guide enthusiastic visitors to a natural communion with wild wolves. On the appointed evening, a well-disciplined convoy of approximately 700 cars set out after sunset to a secret location, deep within the forest, which the rangers had identified as a rendezvous site where adult wolves convene with their fully-grown pups. When a thousand or so people had been silently marshalled into position two of the rangers cupped their hands to their mouths, raised their heads and howled in expert imitation of the wolf's call. As the crowd strained their ears towards the darkened trees for a response, the tension was palpable. After a short wait, the whole pack howled back in a crescendo of sound that rose above the tenebrous forest as if in a

A grey wolf in full voice, one of the most evocative sounds of the wilderness.

LYNN M. STONE

cathedral, enrapturing the human guests. For sound man Trevor Gosling it was the most evocative natural sound that he had ever had the privilege to record.

At two months old a wolf pup waits at the rendezvous site for an adult to return with food.

Most wildlife films contain a sequence or two which, because of their intrinsic difficulty, are shot at the very last moment and only just make it into the final edit. Michelle's research turned up the first of these in Romania where the forests of Transylvania hold the largest remaining popu-

Except in the forests of Romania, European grey wolves are becoming increasingly rare. Nuzzling and licking is a typical submissive gesture which stems from the way wolf pups beg adults to regurgitate their food.

lations of wolves in Europe. On the invitation of Dr Christoph Promberger and Dr Ovidiu Ionescu, leaders of a joint German/Romanian Wolf Research Project, camerawoman Justine Evans and myself went for just two weeks to film some aspects of their work and with luck a wolf or two! We took with us an ultra light-sensitive 'starlight' video camera, in the hope of recording the nightly wanderings of a female wolf, nicknamed Timis, who had been radio-collared by the research team the year before. This year, she had a den in the forest near the old town of Brasov and had eight hungry pups to feed. By regular radio tracking the biologists discovered, to their great surprise, that Timis and her mate divided their hunting activities between red deer in the forest, sheep in the

surrounding meadows and, more often than not, scavenging in the garbage dumps and city bins. The wolves were in fact behaving very much like city foxes in Britain - adapting to whatever food source was easiest to obtain for their families. With the help of the research team, Justine and myself were able to record on video tape the extraordinary sight of Timis nonchalantly crossing main roads and railways to scout the suburbs of Brasov for morsels of fast-food left-overs and other scraps. We even witnessed passers-by giving Timis a cursory glance as if she was no more than a large Alsatian wearing a slightly unusual collar. We wondered whether their attitude would have been quite as nonchalant if they had known that there was a wild wolf in their midst!

*Grey wolves in Canada.
The close bonds of a wolf
pack, reinforced by a variety
of gestures, is the key to
their success as
co-operative hunters.*

*Wolves have excellent eye-
sight, very sharp hearing and
an incredibly sensitive sense
of smell which enables them
to detect prey more than a
mile up-wind.*

The second of these last-minute sequences featured Arctic wolves surviving in the extreme conditions of the far north. We had already mounted two expensive filming expeditions to Greenland which had met with little success since the region's wolves hunt over territories covering 1000 sq. km (625 sq. mls) or more, making them notoriously difficult to follow. But when Dave Mech offered to lead Jeff Turner to a den where parent wolves were raising young pups, we knew that it was worth another try. Dave's secret wolf den was on Ellesmere Island in the Canadian high Arctic where, over the previous ten years, he had carried out research observations and had written a successful book on the subject. And it was here, with Dave's help, that Jeff filmed some of the most amazing sequences of wild wolf behaviour ever seen. These included footage of the two pups emerging from the den for the first time and their subsequent development, the intimate and often endearing relationship between the two parents and the enormous effort required by the adults, the male in particular, to run down and catch enough Arctic hares to keep the pups alive until they could fend for themselves. Another 'nugget' was in the can ready for editing - but only by the skin of our teeth!

JEFF & SUE TURNER

From opposite left:
One of the three week old
Arctic wolf cubs takes an
interest in Jeff's filming.

The Arctic wolf mother
with one of her pups.

The pup solicits food from
its mother.

*An adult wolf can expect little
rest from energetic, six week
old pups.*

LYNN M. STONE

LYNN M. STONE

Wolves are the largest members
of the dog family.

Built for travelling, wolves
can easily cover 80 kms
(50 miles) in a day.

Wolf

Canis lupus

GENERAL DESCRIPTION

Wolves are the largest wild members of the dog family. There are over 30 subspecies of the wolf, *Canis lupus*, world-wide. The following notes refer in particular to the grey wolf, timber wolf and tundra wolf. Adult males average 43 to 45.5 kgs (approx. 95 to 100 lbs) with a maximum of 57 kgs (approx. 125 lbs). Adult females are somewhat smaller, weighing 36 to 39 kgs (approx. 80 to 85 lbs). The male measures 154 to 185 cms (5 - 6½ ft) from the nose to the tip of the tail which is 33cms (*c*. 13 ins) to 51 cms (*c*. 20 ins). The female measures 137 cms (4½ ft) to 182 cms (6 ft) from the nose to the tip of the tail which is also from 33 cms to 51 cms. They stand 66 cms (26 ins) to 91 cms (36 ins) at the shoulders. Their powerful hind legs have large feet with four toes whereas there are five toes on the front paws. Their coat may vary in colour from white, through cream, buff, tawny and reddish grey to jet black.

Built for running they have impressive stamina and often cover considerable distances. Their extremely sensitive sense of smell enables them to detect prey from distances greater than one and a half kms (*c*. 1 mile). In addition they have sharp hearing and good eyesight. The wolf's howl is a well known animal sound that is extremely evocative. Together with the wolf's bark, these vocalisations carry for considerable distances. On the other hand, growling, yapping, whimpering and whining form their close-quarter communications repertoire.

BREEDING AND REARING OF YOUNG

Wolves form long term partnerships, pairing for many years, or even for life. The breeding season is from late January to the end of April, depending upon the latitude. Following a gestation period of around 63 days they produce between one and nine pups (average litter size is four to five) which are born blind and deaf, weighing only about 455 grams (1 lb). Their dens, where this takes place, are excavated beneath tree roots, or in earth burrows, or rock caves. Pups gain 0.91 to 1.36 kgs (2-3 lbs) per week if the mother is in good health and pups are feeding well. After about three weeks the pups appear outside the den and can be observed to act quite playfully, fighting each other and licking or nuzzling the adult wolves' mouths, in seemingly constant pleas for more food. In response the adults may regurgitate half digested food from their stomachs and feed this to their young. The pups are fully weaned after approximately six to eight weeks when they spend more time out of the den and gather at rendezvous sites. The young wolves pass through their juvenile phase from around eleven weeks to one year old by which time they are fully grown. Sexual maturity commences at around 22 to 24 months old.

DAVID WELLING

JEFF & SUE TURNER

JEFF AND SUE TURNER

A lone wolf surveys an area of marshy grassland in Wood Buffalo National Park. Half an hour later she returned carrying a large duck!

MOVEMENT AND FEEDING

They are able to travel great distances and long journeys are almost always associated with their hunt for adequate food. They may cover from 64 to 96 kms (40 - 60 miles) per day and migrating or dispersing wolves are known to have logged up to 800 kms (500 miles) over several days with only brief rests en route.

They are generally meat-eaters, feeding mostly on animals that are larger than themselves, such as deer, caribou, moose and buffalo. The larger the prey the more wolves from the pack are required to bring down the hunted animal and make a successful kill. Smaller animals such as hares can also be chased down and killed. They also scavenge off dead animals and will even turn their attentions to fish such as salmon if they are plentiful or easy to catch. Birds such as ducks may be taken when the opportunity arises. Wolves can store considerable quantities of food in their stomachs, up to 4.5 or 5 kgs (10-11 lbs) may be retained for several days while digestion slowly takes place. They need to drink around 2.25 litres (4 pints) of water per day in order to assist with their digestion.

RESEARCH

Research has focused on several main areas of wolf biology:
• the relationship between selected prey species and abundance with pack size and area of territories;
• dynamics of the pack, including why and when offspring have to find their own territory.

• one recent discovery is the unusual behaviour of Romanian wolves which have taken to behaving more like urban foxes.

CONSERVATION

Historically wolves are the most widespread predator in the northern hemisphere. Constant pressure on them throughout their range has resulted in a greatly reduced population that is now confined to parts of Alaska, Canada, the USA (such as Minnesota and Michigan), and a number of Eurasian countries including Russia, Romania, Italy, Spain, Poland, Scandinavia, Israel, Iran, India and China.

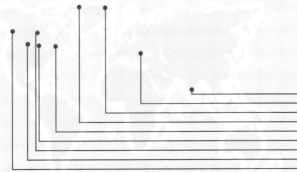

Filming Locations:
Great Bustard Sanctuary, Maharashtra
Brasov, Romania
Northern Greenland
Ellesmere Island
Algonquin National Park
Lake Superior National Park
Wood Buffalo National Park
Nine Mile Valley
Princess Royal Island

Crocodile

KAREN BASS

A Nile crocodile resting on the banks of an African river.

THE GOOD THING about filming crocodiles, I thought, is that they live in warm places. The downside to them is that they don't seem to do very much. Those were my first reactions to the idea of making a 50 minute film about these most ancient of reptiles, survivors from the age of dinosaurs. I was certainly right in believing them to live in hot places; their distribution is almost entirely limited to waterways of the tropics and sub tropics. But my second reaction was thankfully without foundation. One of the greatest rewards of filming *Crocodile* was the opportunity to gain a deep insight into their extraordinary, but secretive lives. In addition it is the closest I will ever come to filming dinosaurs. I felt as though I was on a journey back through time, to an age when these fascinating reptiles shared the planet with their Jurassic cousins. What was so special about crocodiles that had enabled them to survive for over 200 million years when so many other species had failed to do so? The question recurred throughout many months of detailed observation and each new revelation brought me one step closer to finding the answer.

American alligator.

BERNARD CASTELEIN

This was the first film I had made about an animal which could potentially eat the cameraman. Their teeth alone inspired a certain amount of healthy respect! Complacency instilled by their apparent inertia was soon banished as I watched the lightning speed at which they could lunge out of the water to catch an antelope or see off a rival. Calm, still water is no guarantee that crocs don't lurk beneath as they can stay submerged for some hours. The golden rule, I was warned by crocodile scientists the world over, was never to stand too close to the water's edge.

Despite their impressive hunting skills and well-armed jaws they remain, like most wild animals, essentially shy, reclusive creatures. At the first sight of humans they slide down the river banks and disappear under water. The series of hides that we erected on the banks of the Luangwa River in Zambia enabled us to watch and film them unobserved for hours and hours, as they basked in the warm African sun. We were engaged in a long waiting game, and it required patience and perseverance to remain alert for action that did occur. By midday

T. POOLEY

Despite their massive size Nile crocodiles are remarkably agile, even able to catch birds. This individual has snatched a pelican, but will be unable to swallow its meal without the assistance of another crocodile to anchor the prey.

temperatures soared above 40 ° C. As cold-blooded reptiles the crocs use the sun to warm up; but when it becomes too hot they can just slip back into the water to keep cool. Cameraman Richard Kirby had no such option and cooked in his airless hide, while hoping for that special opportunity that would make the painful ordeal worthwhile! Although such daytime vigils were occasionally rewarded by brief bouts of dramatic action it was at night that the crocs really came to life.

The BBC had recently developed infra-red lights and special cameras to film nocturnal animals and we were able to use these to great effect. Infra-red, invisible both to ourselves and to the animals we were trying to film, enabled us to illuminate a

riverbank without disturbing the crocodiles. With this new filming technology we could follow and film their natural behaviour during darkness. It was, however, easier said than done; in order to observe the infra-red illuminated scene we were forced to use heavy night vision goggles which were cumbersome, confusing and uncomfortable. I remember my excitement when I first thought I had seen a croc by a bush and stared at it intently, waiting for it to spring into action only to realise eventually that it was not a croc at all but a fuzzy green rock! But despite these draw-backs our night watches and nocturnal photography of Nile crocodiles at Luangwa revealed some of the most exciting behaviour in the whole film.

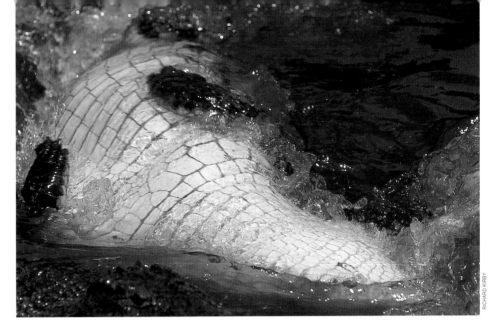

Contradicting the popular belief that Nile crocodile catch the occasional large mammal and then eat nothing for months, research involving examination of stomach contents has revealed that 70 per cent of their diet is in fact fish. Furthermore the research has shown that they are adaptable and opportunistic predators, consuming just about everything from tiny snails, fish and birds to whole buffalo. But when and how do they do this? In Luangwa the night vision cameras really came into their own. During the day a large number of crocs lazed, crowded together, on the banks of a small lagoon which was rapidly drying out. Why were there so many in this seemingly inhospitable site? What were they doing? They posed more questions than we could answer until, that is, we watched them at night. We then discovered that the drying pool had trapped many fish, allowing the crocs to enjoy their own version of a midnight feast! They spent hours fishing, employing different techniques for different situations. One first used his tail to herd the fish into the shallows where, once entrapped, the croc just turned around and made a meal of them. Later that night the same animal stalked cat-like in the water and pounced on an unsuspecting fish. Sometimes they threw their whole body at a fish, lunging at it as if it were a gazelle. Judging by the number of times we actually saw a fish flapping in their jaws as it was being swallowed, there seemed to be many attempted lunges for every successful catch.

We learned that crocs are not just successful predators; they are also opportunistic scavengers. The stench of a dead hippo floating in the Luangwa River was enough to attract crocodiles from miles around. Within a few hours 200 or so had amassed around the carcass and several of them were working as a team in order to devour it. Crocodile jaws are designed as vice-like grips, so the easiest way to break off meat is to grasp tightly and rotate in the water. They literally spin their whole bodies until a bite-sized chunk of flesh is detached. However, this only works if other crocodiles hold the carcass still in the water. To watch 30 or more crocs spin-feeding on a hippo carcass is an extraordinary sight, especially when 150 others are patiently waiting their turn. So many teeth, and so much eating within a small space, and yet we didn't see any hint of fighting.

To consume large prey Nile crocodiles grasp their victim and spin their whole body at great speed to tear off flesh. This only works if other crocodiles are holding the prey steady to prevent it turning.

JOHN DOWNER

Nile crocodiles, like many of the larger crocodilians, are known to take advantage of the habitual behaviour of their prey, taking up position in the water on regularly used game trails, or at well-used river or drinking spots. This topi entered the water once too often.

Lurking low in the water amongst weed the presence of an American alligator in any pool is almost undetectable. But with eyes, ears and nose just above the surface it can see, hear and smell any potential prey.

A Nile croc, filmed in the Luangwa Valley of Zambia, walking out of the water. The high walking posture of crocodiles is more reminiscent of many mammals than of the sprawling gait of most reptiles.

RICHARD KIRBY

84

BBC NATURAL HISTORY UNIT

Infra-red night footage of crocodiles with lions at a carcass. The scent of flesh will sometimes entice crocodile to emerge to feed on land. At night in the Luangwa Valley in Zambia these crocodiles were even prepared to take on lions to steal part of their kill. The pictures were taken with an infra-red sensitive video camera so as not to disturb the animals.

Some time later we were to capture an even more remarkable example of scavenging and co-operative feeding at this same location when we managed to film crocodiles actually stealing meat from another major predator. A pride of lions had made a kill and a large number of crocodiles had gathered in the shallows close to the carcass. To our astonishment they left the water after dark, marched up to the kill and started to eat right next to the lionesses. The lions seemed as surprised as we were and there were some dramatic moments between two of Africa's top predators. At the same time hyenas hung around in the background but didn't dare to take them on. We wondered who would win. Surely one

would drive off the other. But, remarkably, the carcass was finally shared by both lions and crocs, the crocs using a tug-of-war technique to tear off bite-sized chunks.

I was quite familiar with the image of crocs lunging from the water to grasp, wrestle, and eventually consume some hapless gazelle or wildebeest that had timidly approached the river to drink; but I had not fully appreciated their vast repertoire of hunting techniques, nor the tremendous energy employed in such kills. While filming the migration of zebra in the Masai Mara in Kenya, we camped at one of their favourite crossing places on the Mara River. After 18 days spent patiently waiting on the banks of the flooded river we were

Wherever crocodiles live it is dangerous for animals to venture close to water even for a brief drink. This croc has grasped an unfortunate wildebeest by its sensitive nose and will be able to drag it underwater with the minimum risk and expenditure of energy.

The annual migration of wildebeest and zebra across the Mara River in Kenya is a potential bonanza of food for the resident crocodiles. But the large numbers make it difficult to select a target and usually it is only the weakest and smallest that get caught.

Once a kill is made other crocodiles quickly home in on it. An individual would be unable to defend such a large meal and in fact several crocodiles co-operatively feeding on a carcass make it easier to break it up into bite sized chunks. They will consume the whole body, hooves and all. Crocodiles have some of the most powerful digestive juices in the animal kingdom.

beginning to despair of ever seeing a zebra put a hoof in the water. But finally it happened. One morning there was a tangible sense of excitement in the area. Zebras had amassed in some numbers, a couple of hundred or so, and were braying and snorting and looking at the water. One wrong move could be fatal. The massive 5 metre (c. 16 ft) crocs stealthily took up their positions beneath the river bank, motionless and out of view of the zebras.

Eventually three zebras entered the water, braying and snorting as they fought the current. The crocs, power-driven by their massive tails, sped towards the zebras who were unaware of their presence. Suddenly there was an almighty splash as a croc lunged out of the water and, with its huge jaws, attempted to grab a zebra's haunch. This is both difficult and dangerous for the crocodile.

A kick from the zebra can mean a broken jaw and a crocodile with a broken jaw will probably starve to death. Nearly all adult zebras that the crocs attempted to catch escaped. Their backsides were just too large to grab hold of securely. Foals, however, were a different matter. Within minutes, the hunters had turned their attention to these easier prey. One minute a foal was swimming behind its mother, the next it had disappeared, grabbed by the neck and dragged beneath the water. In an instant both prey and predator had vanished.

Crocodiles are not just hunter killers but scavengers also. Here, in the Luangwa valley in Zambia, they are devouring the carcass of another croc which probably died of disease or old age.

American alligator swimming underwater at Silver Springs Florida. Power is provided by the undulating beat of its long sinuous tail. Bony scutes are arranged to ensure the most efficient flow of water over the body and tail.

PETER SCOONES

In order to film underwater we were forced to leave the turbid, muddy waters of Africa and fly to Florida where clear, fresh springs inhabited by another crocodilian, the American alligator, provided a perfect opportunity to observe their swimming. But fully-grown alligators have been known to attack people so we had to find a means of filming underwater in safety. To do this we opted for a small underwater video camera mounted on the end of a 3 metre (10 ft) pole. Sitting in a small boat directly above a large alligator may not be the most comforting of occupations but the resulting footage provided a fascinating insight into an alligator's watery world. Our filming vividly portrays the graceful sinuous movements of the enormous reptile's powerful tail propelling it at speed through the water. The hydrodynamic arrangement of bony scutes on its back and tail streamlines the body and aids efficient propulsion. We were also fascinated to watch how it used its webbed hind feet for swimming and to aid balance when hanging suspended in mid water. Despite their somewhat clumsy gait on land, all crocodilians certainly have a wonderful mastery of the aquatic environment.

Alligators are well known for the loud bellowing which they give voice to during the breeding season, as part of their courtship ritual. When the males emit their penetrating bellows, their whole bodies vibrate, causing the surrounding water to dance and creating the impression of dozens of little fountains spurting over their backs. Apart from the audible sound, which can be heard throughout the swamp, recording with hydrophones has revealed a subsonic repertoire beyond the range of our normal hearing. Given that sound travels faster, and generally further, through water than through air, these signals are yet another way that males declare their presence in an attempt to persuade other males to keep their distance while having the opposite effect on females.

Alligator floating at the surface. To submerge, the alligator changes its profile by bringing its limbs in against the body into a torpedo-like shape. Internally, a system of muscles shift both the liver and the stomach that contains a ballast of sand or pebbles, which alters the reptile's specific gravity. This enables the lungs to expand and thereby store more oxygen so that the alligator can stay submerged for some hours.

An American crocodile basking with mouth open. Compared to the scales and armoured scutes on the rest of their body, the mouth is the most vascularised and permeable part of their skin. Crocodile tongues have numerous blood capillaries and may play a role in temperature regulation.

When swamps dry up mud is a vital buffer against rising temperatures for American alligators. It keeps their skin cool and also discourages parasites.

KAREN BASS

T POOLEY

Cameraman Richard Kirby filming the hatching of baby Nile crocodiles in Natal, South Africa. The mother is close, and at this time is most protective and potentially aggressive, so this is a tense moment.

Crocodilian social life is most apparent during the breeding season. Fighting between rivals and courtship displays are dramatic but unfortunately for us, they are largely unpredictable. The dominant male in any group is the one to watch. Males are distinguished from females by their more prominent ear turrets, head crests behind the eyes, and larger snouts. Once the dominant male has been identified, usually by the fact that he is the biggest and most monstrously magnificent creature in the pool, it is a question of just watching and waiting. To add to our frustration we could frequently hear excited splashing sounds coming from inaccessible locations. When we were lucky enough both to see and to hear these dramatic and noisy displays we learned that the splashes were caused by male crocodiles slapping their heads hard against the water surface to create shows of strength that presumably impressed the more gentle females and warned off rival males.

Nile crocodile females guard the nest for 90 days, caring for their eggs and offspring in a most impressive manner. In order to film the hatchlings emerging from their shells

The temperature gradient within the nest determines the ratio of male to female hatchlings. Over hot summers the majority will be males which are heavier and larger at birth than females.

At birth baby crocodiles are miniature replicas of adults and within days will be hunting for themselves.

we had to know precisely when the eggs were laid. With such maternal dedication on the part of the crocodiles, we could hardly complain about our own long vigils at the nesting sites. The first indication that something was about to happen was the evocative sound of unborn hatchlings, chirping from underground. In response to these plaintive cries for help the female rubbed her throat against the ground and began to excavate the nest. Sand and rootlets flew everywhere and slowly the eggs were exposed. The outer shell cracked and a snout pushed against a pliable inner membrane. It was a tense time for Richard Kirby as he tried to capture the exact moment the hatchling pierced the case with its egg tooth and then slithered into the world. One of the most magical moments of the entire film, it was also one of the most dangerous for the cameraman. A mother crocodile will stop at nothing to defend her young, especially at this, their most vulnerable time. In order to remain as unobtrusive as possible we used a combination of techniques. Long focus lenses enabled Richard to cover the action without intruding on the scene; whilst the hatchling's view of their mother, as she excavated the eggs and tended the baby crocodiles, was filmed with a tiny 'lipstick' video camera which we had earlier buried in the sand among the eggs.

DAVID KJAER

A mother's head is the safest place to bask for this young American alligator. While they are small they are very vulnerable to predation and remain with their mother for protection for several months.

A Nile crocodile hatchling. From the earliest age they stalk insects, frogs and other small animals, while remaining amongst the relative protection of vegetation in the shallows.

Maternal care in female Nile crocodiles is remarkable. The mother picks up any unhatched eggs and, rolling them gently between her tongue and palate, cracks them open to help the babies hatch.

T POOLEY

The newly born young attract their mother with yelping calls. She pushes her head into the nest and carefully picks them up between her sharp teeth. Transporting up to 20 at a time, she then carries them to water and washes them out with a gentle side to side motion of her open mouth.

KAREN BASS

If not disturbed by potential predators, such as monitor lizards, the Nile crocodile mother scoops the tiny hatchlings into her mouth, one by one, until her throat pouch bulges with a dozen or so. Then she lumbers down to the water's edge and washes them out into their new aquatic home. When all 30-40 have been successfully transported she will then spend another month or more guarding the entire crèche. It seemed that her 'fellow' crocodiles were as much a threat to the hatchlings as any other predator. More than once the mother we were filming saw off a passing female who approached too close for comfort.

One of the last shrinking pools, as the Venezuelan Llanos dries up, is home to a concentration of spectacled caiman.

RICHARD KIRBY

Caiman mothers of the llanos wetlands in Venezuela are faced with the additional problem of protecting their babies as the pools dry up around them, necessitating an almost constant search for new water. Each time a rippling pool becomes a sticky mud bath it is time for the caiman and her young to move on. Once again our infra-red camera came into its own, enabling us to record the nocturnal journey of a mother caiman and her brood on this survival mission. They travelled in a procession, traipsing through dry grasses and woodland in search of water. When pools became scarce, several families ended up together. While the resident mother often saw off new females she sometimes adopted the newly arrived babies, boosting the number of babies in her care to the extent that 100 or more youngsters of different ages might be found together in a single pool. These fascinating South American caiman care for their young for at least five months, longer than the parental care period of any other crocodilian.

RICHARD KIRBY

98

MARK DEEBLE & VICTORIA STONE (OXFORD SCIENTIFIC FILMS)

A six to eight week old Nile croc lazing on its mother's huge foot. From hatchling to adult, a crocodile's body weight increases from between 2000 to 4000 times.

These jaws can be closed with incredible force by the massive muscles at their base. The large canines have sharp cutting edges, and are well adapted to puncturing and gripping prey. All the teeth are regularly replaced by new ones growing beneath.

After ten months spent filming crocodiles my respect for these ancient reptiles has considerably deepened and I have begun to appreciate the reasons for their global success. Watching them in action I now realise how well they are suited to the habitats in which they live. The fossil record indicates that the order of crocodilians has undergone no significant structural alteration for about 60 million years, suggesting a unique formula for success, and one that has endured since the days of the dinosaurs. They are far more than just superb hunting machines. I enjoyed a privileged view of them as highly adaptable and social creatures, certainly not primitive reptiles. But I was also surprised at how little we really know and understand them. Our night-time filming revealed fascinating new perspectives on their behaviour, but even this additional insight was only a glimpse into their extraordinary lives, a brief window into the age of the dinosaurs.

The caiman has the most extensive dorsal armour of any crocodilian. Behind the massive bony head are thick ossified scales on its back and neck.

The salt water crocodile lives in a whole range of habitats, from isolated billabongs to freshwater rivers and swamps, brackish estuaries, mangrove areas, and even the open ocean. They have colonised much of the Indo-Pacific region. Their ability to tolerate saltwater is due to salt glands on their tongue which can excrete excess salt.

ROSS COOPER-JOHNSON

P. LAWSON

Saltwater crocodiles have conquered the open ocean and are sometimes found several hundred miles out to sea.

R.KIRBY

P. LAWSON

Crocodile

Crocodylus niloticus, Crocodylus porosus, Gavialis gangeticus, Alligator mississipiensis, Caiman crocodilus . . .

CARL R. ENGLANDER

GENERAL DESCRIPTION

Crocodiles are the largest living reptiles and there are 23 crocodilian species throughout the world, living in tropical and sub-tropical areas in aquatic habitats. *The Wildlife Special, Crocodile*, filmed just five of these species, i.e. the Nile crocodile *(Crocodylus niloticus)*; the Indopacific crocodile *(Crocodylus porosus)* which is also known as the saltwater or estuarine crocodile; the gharial *(Gavialis gangeticus)*; the American alligator *(Alligator mississipiensis)*, and the common caiman *(Caiman crocodilus)*.

The Nile crocodile is not restricted to the river Nile but occurs in many areas of sub-Saharan Africa and Madagascar. Males reach 6 m (*c.* 20 ft) in length. The Indo-Pacific crocodile is the most widely distributed, occurring in Australia, Bangladesh, Brunei, Burma, Cambodia, China, India, Indonesia, Malaysia, Palau, Papua New Guinea, Philippines, Singapore, Sri Lanka, Solomon Islands, Thailand, Vanuatu and Vietnam. Along with the gharial, this is also the largest crocodilian at up to 7 m (*c.* 23 ft) in length and with a reputation as a man-eater. It possesses well developed salt glands on the tongue enabling it to survive in a saltwater environment. 'Salties', as they are commonly referred to, often swim along the coastline when moving from one estuary to another. Although they have been seen on coral-reefs they are not normally resident there but may be en route to a new estuarine location. They tend to be quite solitary in their existence, intolerant of each other, but in other ways they display more typical crocodilian behaviour.

The gharial is found in Bangladesh, Bhutan, Burma, India, Nepal, and Pakistan. Males may grow up to 7 m (*c.* 23 ft) long. It is the most aquatically adapted crocodilian, with heavily webbed rear feet and highly developed scutes along the tail, but is less well adapted to locomotion on land with relatively weak front legs. The gharial's main diet is fish and it has a long slender snout which helps in catching its food. Males develop a bulbous nasal appendage. It is less noisy than some other species, but emits a variety of hisses and snorts, while the male produces a buzzing sound through the snout.

Post-natal care has been observed, although gharial do not carry their young from the nest, presumably because their elongated snouts are less suitable for this purpose than, for example, the Nile crocodile's shorter and more robust snout.

The American alligator lives in the southern region of the United States and is one of the most studied species. Adults may reach 4.5 m (*c.* 15 ft) in length. It principally inhabits swamps and marshes, although it can occur in other habitats, including, on rare occasions, the ocean. It is a very vocal crocodilian, especially during the mating season in April and May, possibly as a result of living in dense vegetated habitats in contrast to quieter crocs that live in more open environments. Alligators have been observed in winter surviving in frozen ponds with their snouts pointing out through the surface. They keep their bodies at a 45° angle, utilising the higher temperatures of the deeper water, and adjusting their metabolisms to a minimal maintenance mode. At such times their body temperatures can be as low as 5°C.

The common caiman, also known as the spectacled caiman, occurs naturally in Brazil, Colombia, Costa Rica, Ecuador, El Salvador, French Guiana, Guatemala, Honduras, Mexico, Nicaragua, Panama, Peru, Suriname, Trinidad and Tobago, and Venezuela. In addition it has been introduced to Cuba, Puerto Rico and the United States. Adults are usually about 2.5 m (*c.* 8 ft) in length. It is a very adaptable species, presently occupying habitats previously dominated by other crocodilians, and it readily inhabits man-made environments, leading to problems with feral populations. In the dry season caiman congregate in isolated ponds in the Venezuelan llanos where the densely stocked shallow pools give the impression of wall to wall caiman. During our filming we counted 200 adults living in a 50 m (*c.* 162 ft) diameter, 2 m (*c.* 6 ft 6 ins) deep pool.

Crocodilians communicate through use of a combination of sounds and body postures, the former ranging from grunts and coughs to loud bellows; the latter comprising arching of heads and tails together with quite dramatic headslaps. In addition to the penetrating bellow of the American alligator, a sound which echoes through their swampy domain, the adult males also emit a low-

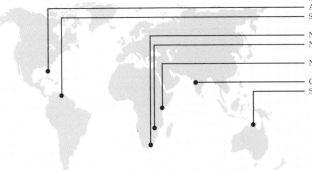

frequency signal, which can be seen, rather than heard, by humans since the vibrations cause water droplets to 'dance' along their backs. Bellowing occurs throughout the year but is most common during the courtship season, from April to June.

BREEDING AND CARE OF THE YOUNG

Riverine species such as the Nile crocodile and gharial tend to nest in holes in, or close to, the river bank. Sand banks provide natural nest sites when water levels are low, during the dry season. Saltwater crocodiles, alligators and caiman build nest mounds, creating patches of relative dryness among their swampy and marshy habitats. In this case suitable materials and sites tend to be found in the wet season. The American alligator's present range, in a temperate to sub-tropical area, necessitates breeding during summer and they therefore have quite short breeding seasons. In Florida for example the entire population of females lay their eggs within a two week period of June. Crocodilians do not have sex chromosomes but the temperature of the embryo in the egg determines the sex of the hatchling crocodile. Nest temperatures of 32-34°C in alligators produce males while temperatures of 28-30°C produce females.

Caiman maternal care is possibly the most extended of all crocodiles. The young hatch at the commencement of the dry season, as the pools are drying up. The mother will often lead a line of young crocodiles from one pool to another across open savannah. When females clash in small pools the dominant female is often left with another's brood. Females with young from eight nests have been observed. One to two year old juveniles also mix with the parents and recent offspring, creating a mixed group.

FEEDING

Crocodiles are slow growing creatures with low metabolic rates, extremely efficient at converting food to body weight. Feeding frequency diminishes with age and older crocodiles can survive on very little food intake. Unlike warm blooded mammals they do not require huge quantities of food and can survive on a meagre diet of fish, crabs, birds etc. An adult may be 100 times longer and several thousand times heavier than a hatchling. Maintenance costs per gram of tissue are much lower for a large crocodile compared to a small one, but the performance capacity of a small croc is much greater. Following a large burst of energy the recovery period for a large crocodile is more likely to be several days than a few hours. A one tonne crocodile may last for up to two years without a meal. On the other hand they will eat almost anything and their stomachs are the most acidic on record for any vertebrate, allowing them to digest all the bones that they eat.

Reptiles have comparable metabolic rates that are only about one tenth those of a bird or mammal of equivalent size. Their low energy consumption is matched by notable efficiency in converting that energy into biomass. An alligator, for example, converts 40 per cent of food eaten into body mass, compared with less than 3 per cent for birds and mammals.

CONSERVATION

In 1971 all 23 species were endangered, depleted, or declining. In 1992 11 species remain endangered, seven critically so, seven can now sustain a regulated harvest, and five species have stable or increasing populations. In 1996 Australia's population of saltwater crocodiles was reclassified by the U.S. Fish and Wildlife Service from endangered to threatened, a less restrictive designation under the U.S. Endangered Species Act.

Filming Locations:
American Alligator, Florida.
Spectacled (Common) Caiman, Llanos, Venezuela.
Nile Crocodile, Natal, South Africa.
Nile Crocodile, South Luangwa Nat. Park, Zambia.
Nile Crocodile, Masai Mara Nature Reserve, Kenya.
Gharial, Chambal River, India.
Saltwater Crocodile, Northern Territory, Australia.

Leopard

AMANDA BARRETT

Four Spot preferred to hunt at night, taking advantage of his acute eyesight.

Author Amanda Barrett using a red light at night.

OWEN NEWMAN

WITH PUPILS CONTRACTED to hard dots in the hot Zambian sun, the male leopard ambled nonchalantly in our direction. His fur shone warm gold, apricot and chestnut. Velvet black rosettes stretched tightly over a stomach which, full of impala, swung gently from side to side. Just feet away from us, he lay down with an effortless elegance in the dappled shade and was soon fast asleep. In the open car, with our nostrils, skin and hair clogged by African dust, and our eyes strained and tired, we watched, mesmerized by our good fortune, as this, one of the most elusive cats in Africa, lay resting on his side, his head lolling on the ground. A paw twitched, while his heavy flanks rose and fell in the heat. Dust puffed in sudden spurts from a triangular nose still pink with youth. Caught in a ray of sun, long, stiff, white whiskers gleamed and, almost hidden from view, translucent ivory claws were illuminated by the beam of light. Suddenly he woke up, panting heavily. He looked at us with a hard but blank intensity, got up and returned to his kill in the tree nearby. For Owen and myself, this was no ordinary male leopard but one we had come to know and admire for his individuality, his character and his boldness. He had a distinctive pattern of spots above his eyes and, lacking originality or wit, we called him Four Spot.

It was our fifth year of filming leopards for the BBC's Natural History Unit in Zambia's South Luangwa National Park. We had already completed one programme for the *Wildlife on One* series, experimenting, for the first time in Africa, with a very low light level video camera. This was a move away from traditional night-time filming which, in general, used film cameras in conjunction with very strong white light. However, after two seasons we felt that a whole range of leopard behaviour still eluded our cameras, even with the use of our weak lights.

OWEN NEWMAN

Owen Newman using a camera adapted for filming with infra-red light.

Our new mission, thanks to the generous permission of the Ministry of Tourism in Lusaka and the National Parks' Authority in Chilanga, was to make a Wildlife Special that truly entered the leopard's night-time world. To accomplish this daunting task we intended to film in total darkness, using a system of infra-red lights which operate on wavelengths unseen either by us or by the animals that we were filming. The resulting black and white images reveal the atmospheric nocturnal, almost ghostly, world in which the leopard is at its most active. Our infra-red lights were far less obtrusive or disruptive than white light, enabling us to discover, and for the first time ever to film, some sophisticated twists to leopard behaviour.

It proved to be easier said than done. The necessary equipment was cumbersome, goggles used to see the infra-red light were primitive and uncomfortable, the ground was the roughest we had ever driven over, and the thorny thickets were indeed thick and extremely thorny. Using the awkward infra-red, while also attempting to follow and film one of Africa's most secretive cats, gave to the phrase 'working in the dark' a whole new meaning. On average we didn't film anything worthwhile more than once a fortnight, which left many cold, long, hard nights with little or nothing to show for our efforts. After some months our sense of humour had almost evaporated into the hot African air. The cars protested, the cameras groaned, lenses squeaked, the recorder blinked and died. Our sense of deep frustration was barely mitigated by the fact that we were working in one of the most beautiful places in the world.

From the air, you can see the Luangwa river unwinding in majestic loops which carve so sinuously through the landscape that in places it seems almost to be doubling back on itself. It is a wide, brown river that, during a good rainy season, rises many feet and floods the surrounding area. On each bank there is a broad band of thick riverine forest with tall, stately ebony groves and huge mahogany trees together with rain and fig trees, potato bushes, jasmine (whose scent pervades

A female leopard feeds, looks after and protects her cubs with no help from the male.

ANUP SHAH

Even a small cub can be left alone for many hours whilst her mother is hunting.

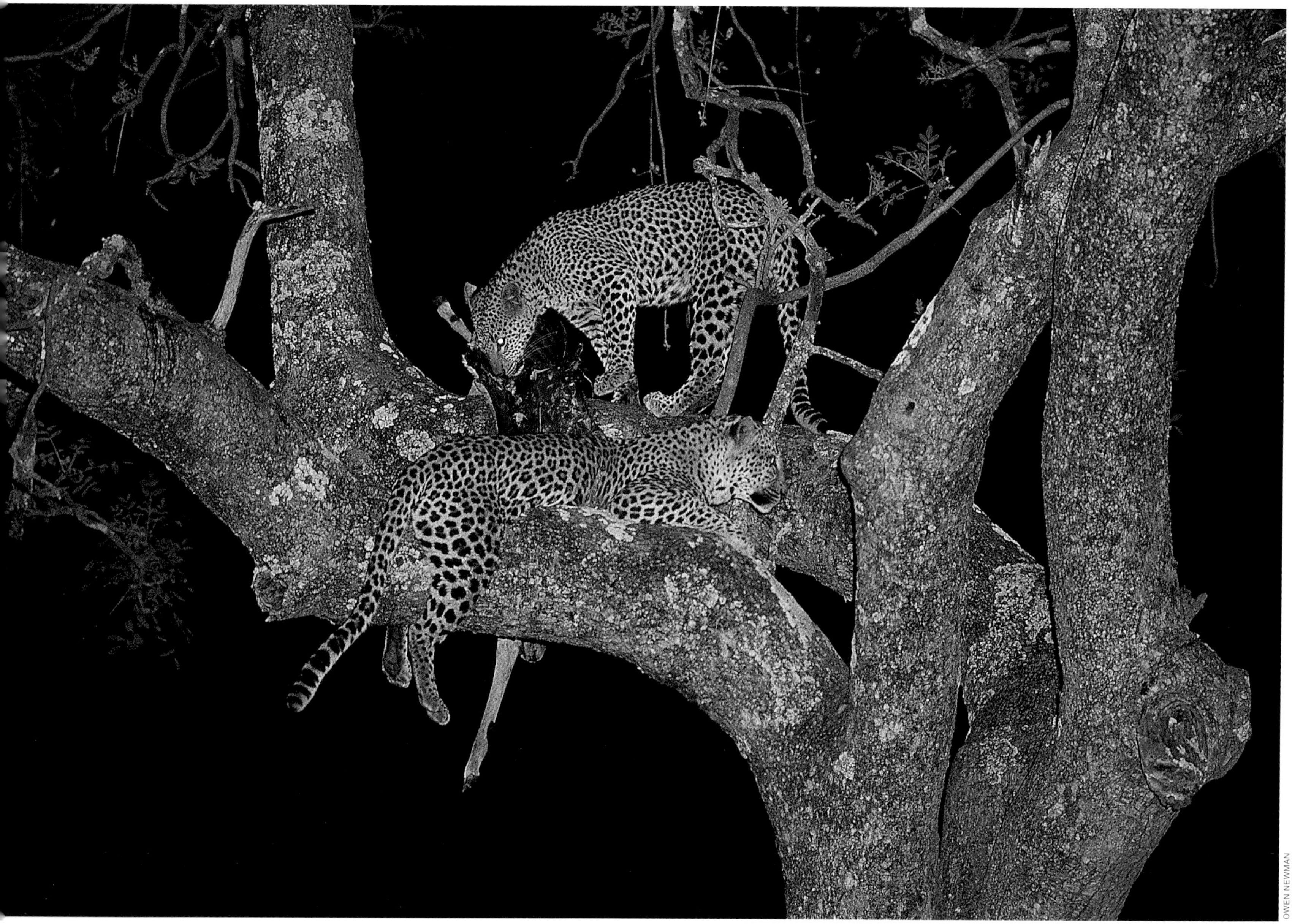

OWEN NEWMAN

the warm night air) and acres of *combretum* thicket. Within the extensive boundaries of the wildlife park, narrow roads follow the river's course, crossing dry oxbow lagoons and threading their way through magical ebony groves which dance with ever moving patterns of light and shade. From May onwards, as the dry season progresses, more and more animals are drawn to the river. Elephant, impala, zebra and puku browse and graze amongst the trees. Fish eagles call from the highest branches and hippos grunt from the river. This is the best time to film leopard, before October, when the temperatures rise too high.

We were especially attracted to this location for night filming because safari companies operating in South Luangwa National Park had, for some time, been running nocturnal excursions. As a result of these, leopards had gradually become acclimatised to the movement of vehicles during darkness. One of the leopards, called Marmalade by the guides, was easily recognisable by a large and persistent wound on her side. This wound, possibly the result of a baboon bite inflicted several years previously, did not seem to have affected the 15 year old leopard too seriously.

We soon realised that our regular working area was limited by the vegetation; too much thicket makes filming impractical so we concentrated on the dry lagoons and groves in one small

sector of the park known as Mfuwe. We were able to persuade an ex-driver/guide, Vernon Baillie, to join us by rashly promising him the most amazing leopard sightings that he could ever imagine. Vernon's knowledge of the birds, animals and plants of the park is drawn from a life-time's experience and a deep interest in nature. He was responsible for operating the lights from a second car and as we bumped and trundled through the steep gullies, trying to find a way through *mopane* stumps that could rip his oil sump apart, his enthusiasm for the task remained surprisingly intact. During ten months of filming, spread over four years, we gradually fulfilled our promise to Vernon.

The main female character, Marmalade, with her male cub who was about a year old but still completely dependent on her for food.

Vernon Baillie operating the infra-red lights.

OWEN NEWMAN

OWEN NEWMAN

Four Spot did most of his hunting at night and usually carried his prey to a safe place where other predators and scavengers could not steal it.

OWEN NEWMAN

Both sexes scent-mark and every leopard has its own, very different character.

As soon as we started filming we realised that unlike leopards in much of Africa, where shortage of food forces a single animal to wander over hundreds of square kilometres, Luangwa's leopards are able to share much smaller territories. In our 50 sq. kms (20 sq. mls) of working country, Marmalade, the wounded leopard, seemed to overlap hunting grounds with another female known as Kumi and a third female whom we nicknamed, for obvious reasons, the Guinea Fowl Hunter (or GFH). We also regularly saw three different males here and a fourth arrived to mate with Kumi. There could easily have been others that we never saw.

For the most part, the different leopards kept their distance from each other and we only observed interactions between non-mating adults when Kumi and GFH met on two separate occasions. On the first occasion, GFH walked past Kumi who merely looked at her with interest. However, the second time we saw them meet, Kumi chased GFH up into a tree where she remained for an hour or so before slinking back down to the ground. Kumi, who had been dozing lightly nearby, woke and chased her into the thickets. Both leopards then walked in different directions, conspicuously marking prominent points by spraying urine, rubbing their cheeks on bushes, and raking tree trunks with their front claws.

When not engaged in mating activity or raising their cubs, leopards lead quite solitary lives. When Kumi came into oestrus, her scent attracted a male whose first response was one of aggression rather than love-making. Although she displayed her female charms, tantalising him by rolling luxuriously on the ground and rubbing her body alluringly against trees, it was obvious, as the male came closer, that he was still dangerously aggressive. They made several passes at each other and on each occasion, right at the last minute, Kumi took refuge up the nearest tree, often perching precariously among the thinnest of canopies, swaying on the fragile twigs. The male waited in the shade for her to descend whereupon the whole emotionally-charged performance was replayed. This pre-courtship game lasted for over two hours and it was difficult for us to follow all their sudden sprints through the thicket. Eventually, however, aggression turned into mutual attraction and, heralded by a cacophony of snarls and growls, they mated. Once the two animals had accepted each other they were loathe to separate and mating took place every few minutes throughout the day and all the following night. Occasionally this intense sexual regime was temporarily interrupted by brief bouts of stalking but, failing in these endeavours, they reverted to regular mating until, quite suddenly, it was all over and they each moved off in opposite directions.

KEITH SCHOLEY

Once a leopard has stored a kill in a tree, it will spend several days in happy luxury.

OWEN NEWMAN

A familiar silhouette of a leopard with its kill, in this case an impala.

Unusually, baboons featured
quite prominently as a favourite
item in the diets of a few
Luangwa leopards.

OWEN NEWMAN

OWEN NEWMAN

Yellow baboon in Luangwa.
The baboons are preyed
upon by leopards.

The leopards rarely resisted hunting opportunities, but when the going got tough, they quickly gave up. Kumi and Four Spot had mastered the art of baboon hunting which, as Marmalade had found to her cost, can be fraught with danger. Baboons have excellent daytime vision and we once observed over a hundred of the primates chasing Four Spot into a bush. But at night their poor nocturnal sight places the baboons at a disadvantage. They roost in tall, slender trees but leopards are skilled climbers and are easily able to out-manoeuvre the baboons in the dark. We filmed Kumi hunting baboons one night and found out what a struggle it was. For about half an hour, she stalked through the branches and leapt from tree to tree. The baboons became increasingly nervous as they frantically attempted to escape from the danger they could hear but could not see. The pandemonium built up to a crescendo until suddenly one big male lost his balance and tumbled to the ground. Kumi charged down the tree so fast that we hardly saw her move, and jumped on the frightened baboon, grabbing him by the base of his neck. The baboon was almost as big as its aggressor and as he tried to bite back, they rolled over and over and past us in a cloud of dust. Kumi's final victory was quick, bloody and violent, shaking us all.

The bonds between a female and her cub are strong and affectionate.

ANUP SHAH

OWEN NEWMAN

The Ju/Hoan bushmen still survive by traditional hunter-gatherer skills.

The Ju/Hoan have skilfully adapted their bows and arrows as dart guns to help in the ecological study of leopards.

While we were following leopards in Luangwa, news came of a fascinating research project in Bushmanland, Namibia where Philip Stander and Philippa Haden were looking at the ecology of leopards in a semi-arid environment. We paid them a visit and found them building up leopard sightings as a basis for a small-scale tourist industry aimed at benefiting the Ju/Hoan bushmen of the area. The latest technology was being employed alongside the finely-honed traditional tracking skills of the bushmen in order to follow the movements of leopards over hundreds of square miles. The bushmen's ability to decipher the behaviour of an animal from the faintest of tracks in the sand was astounding. Tests run by Philip showed them to be almost 100 per cent accurate. By back-tracking away from a leopard located by telemetry, the bushmen were able to define when, what and how it had last killed. They would then communicate the entire chain of events with graphic mimicry. They were able to identify each leopard from its tracks and could quickly recognise the arrival of a new leopard in their study area. The bushmen were small, lithe, fit and immensely impressive. It was certainly a humbling experience to try to keep up with them. Luckily for us, they were also the most generous of people.

At the end of filming *Leopard* for *The Wildlife Specials*, we had been lucky enough to spend more time than anyone else watching the behaviour of several wild leopards at night and had been privileged to observe and record aspects of their lives that no-one else had ever seen. We had succeeded in taking the first tentative but rewarding steps into a whole new world of darkness where we learned, sometimes to our cost, that leopards are smarter and quicker to turn opportunities to their advantage than we could ever have imagined. As we travelled from the lush forests of Zambia to the searing white dust of Namibia, we also learned at first hand of their tremendous adaptability in such sharply contrasting habitats and our respect and admiration for this, the most charismatic of African cats, soared.

*Both men and women from the
Ju/Hoan can expertly follow the
faintest animal tracks in the sand.*

A hungry leopard is quick to take advantage of any opportunity that might result in a meal, however small.

Cubs need over a year to learn hunting skills from their mother before having a chance of fending for themselves.

Leopards are masters of camouflage.

The tallest, smoothest tree is
no obstacle for the best tree
climber of all the big cats.

The leopard - the
most catlike of cats.

Leopard

Panthera pardus

GENERAL DESCRIPTION

The leopard *(Panthera pardus)* is a large member of the cat family, clearly recognisable from its mottled fur which is formed from a close pattern of black and brown rosettes, set against a ground colour which may vary from a pale creamy colour to darker brown or even orange. The colour pattern provides it with a superbly efficient camouflage and the untrained observer could look straight at a leopard hiding among grass without realising its presence. Mature males are thicker set than females, with heavier jowls and faces.

Leopards are found throughout central Africa (excluding the Sahara desert) wherever there is sufficient cover for concealment; and from the Arabian peninsula through Asia to Manchuria and Korea. They have been exterminated from north Africa and from most of South Africa; 26 subspecies have been described but in nearly all cases there are intermediate forms. They are secretive and elusive creatures whose presence in an area is more often revealed by their tracks, faeces or their calls, than by visual contact. Solitary and territorial, they occupy vastly different home ranges, depending upon the physical terrain and the availability of prey. In East Africa leopard home-ranges have been recorded from as small as only 9 sq. kms (*c.* 3.5 sq. mls) up to 63 sq. kms (*c.* 24 sq. mls). In Namibia, where game is much more sparsely distributed, male leopards have been recorded as occupying territories from 210 sq. kms (*c.* 82 sq. mls) to 1,164 sq. kms (*c.* 455 sq. mls) while females have a smaller range with areas from 183 to 194 sq. kms (*c.* 71-76 sq. mls) being recorded.

FEEDING AND MOVEMENT

Leopards feed on a wide range of prey items, including most antelope species, hyraxes, birds, ostriches, jackals, dogs, baboons, porcupines or almost anything else that they can kill. When hunting larger animals such as antelope they tend to prefer those animals that are no heavier than themselves since, in many cases, the leopard must protect its prey by dragging it to a safe place, often up a tree.

They are most active at night, when they walk throughout their territory, marking their presence by dropping faeces, spraying urine, or by scratching tree trunks with their sharp claws.

BREEDING AND REARING OF YOUNG

In Zambia most matings seem to take place towards the end of the dry season. Leopards tend not to mate for life, but may pair up for relatively brief periods during which courtship is followed by repeated copulation, often more than a hundred in a day or so, after which the animals separate and the female eventually raises her cubs

OWEN NEWMAN

RICHARD DU TOIT

BERNARD CASTELEIN

alone. The gestation period is from 90 to 112 days and up to six cubs are born in a well hidden den, often among dense thicket, or in an excavated burrow or in a cave. The cubs' eyes open after a week but the young remain in their protected hiding place for about six weeks and continue to suckle for three months. They become fully independent at some stage during their second year, when they are also sexually mature. Leopards may live for at least 20 years.

RESEARCH

Since leopards are generally nocturnal and secretive, it is difficult for scientists to observe individual animals in the same way as they are able to study lion and cheetah, both of which are more active in daytime. Most data has been obtained from trapping, and monitoring movements of radio-collared individuals in South Africa. The collaboration between the Ju/Hoan bushmen with Philip Stander and Philippa Haden has led to new insights into the implications of solitary behaviour in an area of low leopard density. A similar study in an area of high leopard density would be invaluable.

During the making of *Leopard* for *The Wildlife Specials*, new information was obtained by using infra-red to watch hunting leopards. In this small area, prey density was high and individual leopards employed a variety of hunting behaviour to outwit antelope: from the classic stalk under cover of darkness where a leopard might take two hours to creep forward 10 m (32 ft 6 ins) or so, to the ambushing technique where a leopard tries to create confusion amongst the prey by running through the middle of the herd and then crouching down waiting for the unwary to blunder past. This last manoeuvre depends on the antelope not being able to see as well in the dark as the leopard.

Filming Locations:
South Luangwa National Park, Zambia.
Bushmanland, Namibia.

Eagle

MICHAEL RICHARDS

THERE WAS NO MISTAKING the rumbling noise and the vibrations that accompanied it. The sense of uneasy premonition that had dragged me from my slumbers half an hour earlier was reinforced now as the ground itself began to shake. I felt as though I was in the grip of a particularly vicious hang-over as the rainforest rattled around me. The earthquake struck at 3.30 am and continued to rattle the rainforest for what seemed like a very long 45 seconds. Lying in my tent, surrounded by majestic trees, there was nothing I could do and nowhere I could hide. I listened anxiously for the sound of crashing trunks, but none came. Sleep was impossible and as I lay in the dark, I reflected on the task that lay ahead. It was almost time to leave this magical setting and to make the four-hour hike to the forest edge where the helicopter was due to collect us.

We had been drawn here by a most bewitching bird, and one that was heading towards extinction in the wild, with only about 30 pairs remaining in their natural habitat. Our mission to film the Philippine eagle had begun months previously with painstaking preparations that left us wondering whether we would ever reach this point. My companion on this expedition was a professional tree surgeon, Graham McMahon, who had assisted in building a tree platform for the filming hide. Despite the triumph of placing both myself and equipment within close range of an eagle's nest it had been a long waiting game before the cameras finally rolled on one of these magnificent birds approaching its nest.

The Philippine eagle is the rarest, most endangered, and one of the largest eagles in the world. Its huge size, massive wingspan and bizarre plumage create a striking presence and a sense that this is undoubtedly the master of its rainforest home. Given their scarcity in the wild and its importance as one of the stars of *Eagle*, we considered every possible means of doing full justice to this enigmatic creature. Our research had thrown up information on a captive breeding programme and we considered whether it might be possible to fly one of these human-adapted birds in its natural habitat. After considerable effort to obtain the necessary permissions, Steve and Emma Ford, from the British School of Falconry, spent six gruelling weeks training Kali, a seven-year old female Philippine eagle, to fly free through the forest, not huge distances, but far enough to give us some wonderful images

NEIL P. LUCAS

Cameraman Michael Richards filming in Singapore with a very helpful Blythe's Hawk Eagle.

A Philippine eagle, one of the most impressive eagles we were lucky enough to see and film.

MICHAEL W. RICHARDS

Stephen Ford with Kali the Philippine eagle which he trained to fly for the film. Being only the second person to train and fly a Philippine eagle in the last 25 years, Stephen took everything in his stride including the eagle's impressive size. Use of trained birds not only kept disturbance of the wild birds to a minimum but also allowed us to obtain some excellent film sequences.

of this very special bird in its natural home. It was the first time such a project had been attempted with Philippine eagles and it provided us with some stunning footage.

The earthquake shook us 1000 kms (625 mls) from where we had filmed Kali, in truly wild territory where some, at least, of the few remaining birds nested. Concealed and patiently waiting within our tree-top hide, we were in surroundings so uncompromisingly remote it was, my Australian colleague remarked, as though we had succeeded in "opening the pages of *National Geographic* and walking off into them". The forest people were as interested in us as we were in the eagles. Fascinated by what they regarded as our beautiful long

noses, they decided that Graham's superb ability in tree climbing was directly attributable to the shape of his nose which clearly breathed in more oxygen than their own, somewhat squashed noses.

A wildlife cameraman is very much dependent upon the support of his colleagues and for this project I was extremely fortunate to be working with a highly experienced production team. Our producer, John Downer, is a master at imagining sequences that will enable the audience to feel just what it is like to be the animal subject of his film. His past series like *Supersense*, combined with his recent work on commercials and feature films, ensured that the content and look of this film was going to be fresh and exciting. John had teamed up with assistant producer Neil Lucas, once a falconer but now one of the most skilful organisers of technically difficult wildlife shoots. Neil is a problem-solver, one of the best supports you could hope for in a difficult situation.

Persistent downpours were what we had expected in this rainforest region but the foreknowledge did not make our task any easier. While the first stage of our journey had been undertaken in relative comfort, aboard two Huey helicopters belonging to the Philippine airforce, the next stage had proved more arduous, necessitating a five-hour hike and 27 porters to help in carrying our equipment. With the assistance of an excellent guide from the PEFI (Philippine Eagle Foundation Incorporated) we eventually managed to reach the chosen site, nearly two months later than originally planned.

Gaining access to the filming hide was not easy. First it was necessary to negotiate, under the protection and confusion of darkness, an almost vertical slope, guided by a 100 m (325 ft) fixed line, to the base of the hide tree. Next I had to haul myself up the 25 or so metres (80 ft) of rope and clamber into the hide - an effort which invariably left me steaming with perspiration. Because moisture clings to anything metal, I could never unpack the camera until I had cooled down.

MICHAEL W. RICHARDS

138

Some of the 27 porters crossing a
river on the walk through the
forest to the wild nest site.

In addition to the physical effort there was a particularly powerful emotional element to my vigil in the hide. The quiet atmosphere of the pre-dawn forest mesmerized me as soon as

Philippine eagle.

NEIL P. LUCAS

I was alone and a sublime feeling of awe and wonder flooded the soul. Hidden, motionless and silent, I strained my ears for the sounds of nature - clues to what action I could expect. Almost shaking with excitement, the sense of anticipation kept me alert throughout the day for nobody had filmed these birds in the wild during the previous 20 years. The opportunity to film the adult eagle tending to its two month old chick might come only once, and I must be ready for that moment.

As with other nest-site vigils, the first visit by a parent bird proved to be, for me at least, the most electric. The majestic eagle landed at the nest and stared directly at the camera lens, seeming to see through our camouflage. Remaining stock still, I felt her gaze burn through the elements of the lens, fixing on my own eye. Trying hard not to blink, I held my breath and then, finally, and to my huge relief, she turned away. After feeding her lone chick she flew straight towards my hide, a monkey's tail dangling from her beak. What a reward! Despite the apparent closeness of our encounter, enhanced by the camera's powerful telephoto lens, I was in fact 40 m (130 ft) from the nest and the eagle was not disturbed by my presence. She even watched us earlier, from a respectable distance, as we constructed the filming hide. Perhaps the delays worked to our advantage for she was no longer brooding eggs or keeping her chick warm and dry.

140

Clockwise from top left:
African hawk eagle;
Bateleur eagle;
Steller's sea eagle;
Blythe's hawk eagle.

NEIL P. LUCAS

Crowned hawk eagle.

Crowned eagle on nest 28 m (90 ft)

in the tropical rainforest canopy.

MICHAEL W. RICHARDS

JOHN DOWNER

Golden eagle, 'star' of the film.

Eagle was to cover 12 of the world's most spectacular eagles neatly linked in a story whose central character was the golden eagle. Our declared aim was to depict the behavioural and physical characteristics that distinguish each species and link them to the environments in which they live. It was essential that this Special film be dynamic and dramatic, visually stunning and exciting. Above all it had to do justice to the eagles themselves, reflecting their unique charisma. In doing so it would enter uncharted territory, drawing inspiration from their wild habitats and their natural behaviour, showing things that had never before been televised. And finally, it would tell the truth. It was a project that took us to some of the most beautiful and remote places imaginable and the thrills of filming the Philippine eagle were repeated in different ways, in other far flung corners of the globe.

Golden eagles took us to the Alps and Scotland for the opening sequence, and then to Greece where we filmed them eating tortoises. Eagle migration was illustrated by steppe eagles as they flew over Israel and down to Africa. And it was here that we were able to show the great variety of species that live within this evolutionary cauldron. Crowned eagles hunting vervet monkeys in Zimbabwe; the classic African forest eagle; and the black eagle, a close relative of the golden eagle, hunting rock hyrax. We also filmed a wild black eagle

nest with newly hatched chicks engaged in fighting each other to death, the so-called 'Cain and Abel' struggle. Zimbabwe also provided us with sequences of the tail-less bateleur eagle in full glide, and the African fish eagle on man-made lake Kariba and on lake Victoria in Kenya where their unexpected prey includes flamingoes. Another African species we filmed at the nest was a martial eagle which hunts a wide variety of animals.

For sequences of white-bellied sea eagles hunting sea snakes we flew to Malaysia where several pairs live quite close to each other in a section of that country's remaining forest. Their spectacular territorial displays more than justified both the pre-planning that ensured our presence there at the right time of year and the journey itself.

Martial eagle, Zimbabwe.

Crowned hawk eagle, a typical forest hunting bird, well adapted for catching the vervet monkeys that make up part of its diet.

NEIL P. LUCAS

144

Golden eagle on branch, Sweden.

BENGT LUNDBERG

LYNN M. STONE

American bald eagle on perch.

Bald eagles, along the Chilkat
river in Alaska, one of the
world's great eagle spectacles.

JOHN DOWNER

Timing was also a key element in our Alaska trip, which took place in December when frozen ice coincides with still relatively warm river water. It is a time when bald eagles congregate to feed on late runs of spawning salmon. On our first full day there, we rose from our sleep to be greeted by scenes reminiscent of Dante's 'Inferno', with swirling mists hanging over the water like smoke rising from a fire.

Steller's sea eagles took us, in late winter, to icy-cold Kamchatka in eastern Russia, where the salmon were still running and eagles hungry. These magnificent birds have a huge bill which can easily rip open a salmon and our plan was to film them catching and eating the fish. Our Russian guide, Alexander Ladyguin, had studied the eagles for his PhD.

My diary entry for 26 January tells its own story of the trials and tribulations of filming in this harsh environment: "I spoke to Neil on the radio as arranged at 1300 hrs and both he and Alexander thought the wind was becoming too strong, so they wanted to get me out of the hide . . . I was reluctant as the birds were just getting used to its presence and I was slightly sheltered from the worst of the weather. I waited another three hours and had a magpie at the salmon in front of me which I took to be a good sign as they are frequently in the company of eagles . . . Sadly no eagles came and so, with the wind screaming in the trees, I radioed that I was leaving.

MICHAEL W. RICHARDS

Russian helicopter taking off from the shores of Lake Kuril, Kamchatka, one of the more remote locations we visited to film eagles.

KLAUS NIGGE

Steller's sea eagles dispute over food, Kamchatka.

"Neil warned me over the radio that the storm was now intense and the river was breaking up so that it would take them a little longer to reach me. It sounded ominous. When I eventually emerged from the hide the storm hit me with a blast of snow making it impossible to face the wind. Waves battering the lake shore reminded me of a gale-bound sea-coast, and the trek back along the water's edge, dodging the breakers and trying not to be swept away, was a real struggle. The mouth of the river presented a more shocking sight with even more threatening waves and, bouncing around among them, huge blocks of ice on which I could clearly discern our own footprints. In the failing light we donned skis and very nervously crossed the remaining jigsaw of cracks until we safely reached the other side." It wasn't often that we were totally prevented from obtaining any material but this place almost defeated us. On our final day I did manage to film an eagle pulling a live salmon from the water, but it was a meagre return for our efforts.

Steller's eagles in Japan spend the winter accompanying the fishing fleet off the Kuril islands, and, in contrast to the Russian eagles, they displayed no fear of man. Unmolested by hunting, they are proudly protected and their behaviour reflects this fact. As the nets are hauled through the ice-coated sea dozens of Steller's and white-tailed eagles compete between themselves for the fish, creating a striking spectacle alongside jungle crows, slaty-backed and glaucous gulls.

We were extremely lucky to experience such magical light conditions during our filming of bald eagles in Alaska.

Opposite: Steller's sea eagle.

JOHN DOWNER

But the eagles feed in this way only if ice is present. Despite a promising start the ice disappeared on our second day and there followed a long and unproductive period, uncomfortably reminiscent of Kamchatka. Once more facing into the last day with no worthwhile film in the bag, I was beginning to feel that Steller's eagle would be the one to defeat us. A cold, completely calm dawn brought renewed hope. Conditions were once again perfect for filming, but there was one small factor I had forgotten - it was the one Sunday of the month on which no one goes fishing. However, potential disaster was turned to triumph by Mr Ishida who took us out on his trawler especially so we could film. The eagles, having been denied food from the fishing fleet throughout the storm of recent days, were as keen to feed as we were to film them. We watched in wonder as huge Steller's sea eagles descended at high speed, characteristically waggling their wings from side to side and rocking their legs to reduce airspeed, just like a whiffling goose. The agony, pain and frustration of not filming anything for so long gave way to deep relief and surging excitement as the camera whirred and the lens captured many beautiful images and behaviour unique to this particular species of eagle.

Martial eagle, Bulawayo area,

Zimbabwe.

Golden eagle, star of the Wildlife Special: Eagle.

JOHN DOWNER

Verreaux's eagle in its classic habitat of the Matopos, Zimbabwe.

Verreaux's eagle flying over boulders in the Matopo Hills.

JOHN DOWNER

African fish eagle taking fish,

Lake Kariba, Zimbabwe.

African fish eagle.

African fish eagle with kill.

Eagle

Aquila chrysaetos, Pithecophaga jefferyi . . .

GENERAL DESCRIPTION

There are many species of eagles, from the sea- and fish eagles to the golden, tawny and Verreaux's or black eagles and the hawk eagles. The group as a whole is represented by over 60 species and is distributed throughout the major continents of the world with the exception of Antarctica. Different species are adapted in particular ways for their favoured habitats, with some showing greater degrees of specialisation than others. All share excellent eyesight, essential in helping them to locate their prey. Sea eagles and fish eagles possess very rough and scaly feet, providing a firmer grip on the fish that form a key part of their diet. Eagles like the Steller's sea eagle of the east and the bald eagle of America have larger and stronger beaks enabling them to pierce tough salmon skins. Forest dwelling eagles are equipped with broad rounded wings and larger tails, providing enhanced manoeuvrability and the ability to chase their prey between the trunks and branches of their densely wooded domains.

Crowned eagle.

Crested serpent eagle.

One of the largest eagles, the Philippine eagle (*Pithecophaga jefferyi*), stands over 1 m (c. 3 ft 3 ins) high and weighs over 6 kgs (13 lbs), while one of the smallest, the Australian little eagle (*Hieraaetus morphnoides*) weighs only about 480 g (1lb 1oz). Whereas in most birds the male is larger than the female, in birds of prey it is the other way around and a female golden eagle can be almost 30 per cent larger than its mate.

MOVEMENT and FEEDING

The wide variety and range of adaptations found among the eagles is reflected by an equally wide range of prey species. Larger birds such as the golden eagle (*Aquila chrysaetos*) will catch anything from rabbits and hares to small deer, and some of the forest eagles will take tree climbing mammals including monkeys and sloth's, displaying impressive flying skills which enable them to catch their prey without landing. As their name suggests the serpent eagles are adept at seizing snakes and other reptiles. Almost every eagle will feed on any carrion it may come across, whilst some species actively search for carrion, keeping a sharp eye open for the tell-tale sign of vultures or similar birds feeding on the ground. However, not all eagles depend upon live prey or carrion for their food: the African vulturine fish eagle (*Gypohierax angolensis*) regularly eats fruit, and is sometimes called the palm-nut vulture because of its bare face and its consumption of palm-nuts.

BREEDING and RAISING of YOUNG

Breeding habits vary considerably among eagles. In general, however, the average clutch size is from one to four eggs, with the fish and sea eagles tending to lay four whilst the much larger and heavier Philippine eagle lays a single egg. They nest in a wide variety of habitats, depending upon the species, including trees, on mountain tops and even on more level ground. The nest, known as an eyrie, may also range in structure and size. Many of the snake eagles build small flimsy nests in the upper branches of forest trees and may construct a different nest each year. On the other hand most of the larger eagles use the same nest year after year, bringing in new nesting material each season, adding to the existing structure and, over the years, building very large nests. One of the largest recorded bald eagle nests was 36 years old, had a depth of 4 m (13 ft) and a breadth of over 2.5 m (c. 8 ft).

NEIL P. LUCAS

Incubation is normally carried out by both sexes, but where the females incubate alone, the males normally feed their partners on or near the nest. The average incubation period is around 40 days with the Philippine eagle holding the upper record, at 60 days; while the crested serpent eagle (*Spilornis cheela*) of Malaysia has the shortest incubation period at only 28 days. Once the chicks hatch, the parent birds are constantly engaged in hunting and bringing food back to the nest site to feed their ever-hungry offspring. During hard times it may be a problem to feed every chick in the nest and various behavioural adaptations have been noted in connection with sibling rivalry. A dramatic example, known as the Cain and Abel struggle, is provided by the Verreaux's or black eagles (*Aquila verreauxi*) of Zimbabwe, in which the first chick to hatch viciously attacks and kills its day old sibling, thus enhancing food supply for itself and helping to make it as strong and healthy as possible, increasing its chances of survival.

CONSERVATION

For over 4,000 years eagles have been kept and trained by man, as a valued means to obtain food and for sport. For the Aztecs and the Romans they were a symbol of power, and even today many countries like the United States of America and the Philippines have eagles as their national emblem or as their 'national bird', while advertisers throughout the world continue to use them as icons for strength and courage.

For a bird of such importance it has not faired well in its encounters with humans. Increasing pressure to clear land for crops and grazing has placed eagles under threat throughout their range. Being at the top of the food chain they are often in conflict with farmers and other people rearing animals like sheep and goats for food. As a consequence of this apparent conflict with man's interests a variety of 'control' methods have been adopted, including, nest destruction, shooting and the use of poison baits.

As if this was not enough eagles have also suffered, along with other birds of prey, through the side-effects of chemicals applied to the land for pest control. These have made their way through the food chain, concentrating in the top predators such as eagles, with disastrous results for their breeding success, causing some sharp population declines. The chemicals themselves have not directly killed the birds, but their presence in the blood-stream has resulted in weaker eggs with thinner eggshells being laid. As a result many such eggs are crushed or damaged by the brooding parents, while in some cases the chemical pollution has resulted in birds laying infertile eggs. Given the small clutch sizes and the fact that most only lay once per year, or even, as in the case of the Philippine eagle once every two years, any reduction in breeding success can have significant consequences for wild populations.

There are a number of conservation efforts devoted to individual species of eagle. These include a comprehensive breeding enhancement programme for the bald eagle in the United States while the European sea eagle, once exterminated in Britain, is now being re-introduced there. But for some eagles it may already be too late. The Philippine eagle's natural habitat has been decimated to the extent that there are now less than a hundred birds in the wild. Others, like the Madagascar serpent eagle may have recently become extinct, slipping into oblivion unnoticed by man.

Golden eagle.

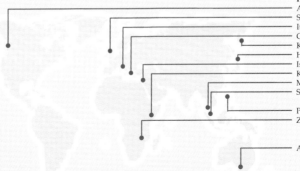

Filming Locations:
Alaska - *Bald eagle*
Scotland - *Golden eagle*
Italy - *Golden eagle*
Greece - *Golden eagle*
Kamchatka - *Steller's sea eagle*
Hokkaido - *Steller's sea eagle*
Israel - *Steppe eagle*
Kenya - *African fish eagle*
Malaysia - *White-bellied sea eagle*
Singapore - *Crested serpent eagle, Blythe's hawk eagle, White-bellied sea eagle*
Philippines - *Philippine eagle*
Zimbabwe - *African fish eagle, Crowned hawk eagle, Martial eagle, Bateleur eagle, Steppe eagle, Black eagle*
Australia - *Wedge tailed eagle*

Whale

ANDY BYATT

The most acrobatic of the great whales, a 40 tonne humpback launches skywards in south-east Alaska. It is the epitome of grace and power.

FEW ANIMALS ARE MORE CHARISMATIC than the great whales and the humpback is possibly the most appealing of them all. Sleek and black, they are extraordinarily graceful, appearing almost to fly underwater on their 4 m (13 ft) outspread pectoral fins. They are also dramatically active - powerful breachers capable of hurling their massive bodies, weighing as much as 60 tonnes, clear out of the water. But their most alluring performances are vocal - the humpback really is the Caruso of the deep, with a song of quite exquisite range and beauty. It is simply the most moving animal call on earth. So not surprisingly the public have embraced the humpback with a fervour, delighting in its size, seemingly peaceful nature and a perception that it possesses great and misunderstood intelligence. Some almost grant humpbacks deity status, surely a creature totally unlike any normal terrestrial mammal?

But these facts are already well known, well recorded and have been frequently televised. Our objective, in making a 'Special' on the humpback was to portray it in a different light and to come back with sequences never before seen on television. The question that arose, as we embarked upon this challenge was, 'did the humpback really have another side to it -that we could film?'

Research on humpbacks, the most studied whale species, has contributed to a changing perception among scientists of whale behaviour. As new evidence accumulates a different picture is emerging: significantly at odds with the popular view of these animals as benign and mysterious giants. Gone is the romantic image of these leviathans calmly cruising the world's oceans like roving peace-makers of the natural world.

A variety of techniques was employed in the making of Whale.

DAVE RUDDICK

Diving humpback in south-east Alaska. Water cascades off shining tail flukes in the late afternoon.

Spy hopping, literally coming half out of the water to take a peek at its surroundings. Large groups of humpbacks congregate to feed in Alaska during summer.

Does whale-watching come any more thrilling than this?

BRANDON D. COLE

In its place we have a more intricate portrait of vast, efficient predators with complex social behaviour, including bloody combat for sexual success. Increasingly it appears that they behave like all of the rest of us mammals - competitive, aggressive and opportunistic.

It was this more accurate perception that producer and cameraman Rick Rosenthal was keen to portray - the concept of the humpback as a hungry and 'hot blooded' mammalian predator. The proposal also appealed to one of the scientists whose research had placed him at the forefront of this revolutionary debate on humpback behaviour, Dr Jim Darling, who joined the project as scientific consultant.

Apart from the challenges of film-making and the creation of dramatic wildlife entertainment programmes for the world's television viewing public, there is a deeper need for us to achieve an understanding of the humpback whale. Virtually all species of whales remain on the endangered list but the simple fact that we no longer hunt many of them is no guarantee of their survival. Unfortunately our impact upon their ocean habitat extends far beyond the direct impact of whaling: commercial fishing still takes a heavy toll, with whales drowning in monofilament gill nets, or having their prime food sources decimated by modern trawlers. Fishing, dredging, mining and pollution also have impacts upon their natural habitats whilst the increase in shipping has altered the harmony of the seas with a cacophony of engine noises travelling considerable distances underwater, distracting marine mammals. If we value whales' presence, and have any interest in protecting their existence, our only hope is to understand the key aspects of their behaviour, not as anthropomorphic pleasantries, but with genuine insight. The filming of 'Whale', we hoped, would create a powerful new impression of humpbacks and raise public awareness about all these issues.

But it would be easier said than done. Both Rick and I had prior experience of making whale films and we both understood the challenges that we would face. The first question was where to get the best results. Humpbacks occur in all the world's oceans and it was essential that we concentrate our efforts where we could make the most of the budget. After careful consideration we decided to focus our attention on the humpbacks of the north Pacific, following them on their journeys from Alaska to Hawaii and Mexico. We would turn to our advantage all the filming and research that had already been conducted on these whales and would work with Jim Darling in the areas where he had the most experience. From a technical viewpoint there was not much that had not already been done but we hoped that by working closely with scientists who had achieved a better understanding of their behaviour, we too would be able to portray them in a more accurate light.

Rick Rosenthal swims with a humpback whale calf.

164

BRANDON D. COLE

A large humpback rockets into the air off the coast of south-east Alaska.

BRANDON D. COLE

Humpback whale off Cabo San Lucas, Baja, after migrating south from summer feeding grounds in Alaska. The whales are in a particularly active mood during their winter sojourn in warmer waters, their breeding season.

Humpback whale shows its pleated throat as it balloons out, filled with water and herring.

Humpback whales 'lunge feeding' in south-east Alaska, explode through the surface as they feast on huge schools of herring during summer months.

BRANDON D. COLE

In June 1996 Rick, accompanied by Jim Darling, commenced filming in south-east Alaska. Humpbacks partake in a dramatic group feeding activity called lunge feeding in which herring are herded into a tight group by a spiralling net of bubbles blown at depth by one or more humpbacks and then, with a massive burst of spray, up to 15 whales lunge out of the surface together, gulping huge mouthfuls of fish in the process. Rick's success in capturing this dramatic activity in riveting close-up, with slow motion shots of whales bursting through panicking herring and appearing as if they were also about to devour the camera, was true pay dirt at the start of the project. My own first view of these exciting scenes was in the safety of an editing suite at the Natural History Unit but, as I later discovered when I joined a subsequent shoot, almost to my cost, the whales did indeed almost devour the camera, cameraman and camera boat!

Close encounters such as these are the life-blood of wildlife filming but they also present the greatest problems. Apart from the sheer physical demands on cameraman and supporting crew, there are many other hurdles to overcome, not least of which is that of obtaining permission to approach these endangered whales since there are strict regulations controlling human proximity to marine mammals in US waters. Unless issued with a permit to do so, it is illegal to purposely approach whales in a boat closer than 100 yards. By working with a licensed cetacean scientist, Dr Jim Darling, we were able to gain the necessary permission.

But permission is one thing; the reality of actually steering a small craft within close range of a large whale, without endangering either the whale or the people on board the boat, is quite another. It requires special skills of boatmanship together with a deep understanding of whale behaviour. Jim has a seemingly telepathic knowledge of where the whales will show up next, combining good judgement with experience and understanding so that time and again he drifted his boat amongst the whales. This intuitive skill is in fact the key to his research work, while for us it provided unique filming opportunities and some incredible shots where the whales appear to lunge into the camera.

To capture these lunge feeding sessions on film it was first necessary to identify the bubbles of a bubble net developing on the surface. Usually once you see that, the whales will appear a few seconds later, bursting into the middle of the net.

The bubbles are, therefore, the cue to start running the camera in order to catch that vital moment when the whales first appear. On one memorable occasion Rick saw bubbles forming alongside the boat. Shouting that the whales were really close, Jim calmly replied: "Actually, we're inside the net!".

A second later they were surrounded by lunging whales, almost grazing the boat's side as their mouths and fins soared up to 4.5 m (c. 15 ft) into the air. Rick hung on with one hand as the boat rocked wildly while with his other he kept the film

Open wide!

DAVE RUDDICK

BRANDON D. COLE

Baleen plates, not teeth, fill the humpback's cavernous mouth. Small fish and tiny plankton are strained through the baleen.

Humpback whale in Frederick Sound, Alaska. Barnacle beard on chin, mouth full of herring that it swallowed during 'lunge feed'.

BRANDON D. COLE

Humpback whales 'bubble-net' feeding, gulping tons of herring they have confused and concentrated by blowing rings of bubbles.

A small pod of travelling humpback whales.

rolling through the camera. It took great balance and steady nerves, but the resulting sequence is one of the most dramatic ever to have been filmed. Particularly so, for the image of one tiny herring that flipped out of the whale's gaping maw just as the jaws clanged shut, and in slow motion tumbled through the air, bouncing off the head of it's immense predator before sliding back into the water. One very lucky herring!

Humpbacks gorge in feeding grounds, like the rich waters of Alaska, throughout the long days of summer, but as the bitter chill of winter returns most of the whales make their way back to the tropics in order to breed. So by February of 1997 our cameras were following the humpbacks to Hawaii

and Mexico where we hoped to film their breeding behaviour and to take advantage of the clear blue tropical seas in order to film whales underwater. The trip provided both the most frustrating time that Rick experienced throughout the filming period and also the most extraordinary coincidence.

He joined Jim Darling and the celebrated *National Geographic* stills photographer, Flip Nicklin, aboard their small research boat - their working base for the next two months. Jim's research was centred on the behaviour of singing male whales and their interactions with any other whales that joined them. It was a slow and difficult task, requiring hours and hours, even days of waiting. For Rick this was extremely testing because he could see general whale activity all around them, all of which would have been worth filming, but the restrictions of permit regulations meant he could only work from Jim's boat and thus had to sit it out and wait for the rare opportunities afforded by the research. It was a classic example of a situation where the best interests of natural history filming and research run in conflict with each other. It was a difficult time for the whole team.

But as in any walk of life patience is rewarded. Eighteen years ago Jim was working with Flip and his father, Chuck Nicklin, in Hawaii. At the time no one believed that it was possible to locate and sex singing whales. One day the team

Humpback whales feed collectively in a process called 'bubble-net feeding'. They encircle a herring shoal with bubbles that form a temporary 'net' causing the fish to concentrate and allowing the whales to lunge through the confused mass of fish, scooping large numbers into their gaping maw.

BRANDON D. COLE

stumbled across a singer - they could even hear the sound of the song clearly through the bottom of the boat. Flip and his father slipped overboard and managed to dive down onto a large whale with a uniquely torn tail. The whale proved to be a male, was later named Frank, and provided something of a milestone in cetacean research - confirming for the first time ever that divers could locate and actually swim with 'singing' whales, taking visual note of their features, including whether they were males or females.

Nowadays it is a matter of routine to locate a singing whale. So one morning the team found themselves drifting above a loud singer. As they waited to see if any other whales would join up, the whale responsible for the recordings came to the surface to breathe and as it dived down flicked a large and uniquely torn tail into the air. Incredibly, after a gap of 18 years, Flip and Jim had stumbled across Frank once more - a hugely exciting encounter - almost like meeting up with a long lost mentor and one that immediately recalled for them the thrill of their first dive with the same humpback all those years ago. Would it be possible to do the same again?

The best method of approaching whales underwater is to snorkel or free dive since they are often irritated by the noisy bubbles of a scuba set. Flip and Rick slid into the water, gulped air and duck dived to begin their descent to 20 m (65 ft). The whale lay motionless in the water, so huge that Rick later described the sensation as approaching a living, parked 747 jet! Like humans, whales have a personal sense of space, how much space they require varies from animal to animal, so divers are never sure how close they can swim before causing the whale to take off into the gloom. For a cameraman this is an agonising moment, with questions like 'Will I get my shot?', 'How much closer can I get?' and 'How much longer can I hold my breath?' tugging at one's conscience while

A playful young humpback whale in south-east Alaska thrashes its flukes during a 'tail-lobbing' show. Young humpbacks are particularly active.

BRANDON D. COLE

Humpback whales underwater. An 'escort' male in the foreground with cow and calf behind. Despite being 12 m (40 ft) long these adults still swim with tremendous grace and harmony.

every effort must be made to focus the camera and make sure that everything is functioning correctly. And after one has managed to overcome all obstacles and actually filmed the whale underwater, there is the rush back to the surface, lungs burning, and still the nagging worry that the camera may not have performed perfectly. It's only after developing the film that you'll know for sure. In this case the nervous suspense was unfounded and Rick produced a beautiful sequence of the old operatic in action.

By June most of the breeding humpbacks had returned north to feeding areas, so we also headed back to south-east Alaska - this time with our sights set on some good aerial shots of the whales and to film the scientists in action. The latter task threw up some interesting moments - not least a memorable encounter with a pack of hunting killer whales.

We had seen a small pod of killers working close to the shore, moving quietly and blowing for air infrequently. Something about their movement suggested that they might be hunting, so we trailed them for over an hour. Suddenly we sighted humpback blows a mile ahead and began to wonder if the killer whales might be hunting them. There were five humpbacks and all of them appeared to be resting - lying motionless at the surface, hardly breathing. The killer whales edged closer and closer. Soon they were scarcely 50 m (160ft)

Mother and calf humpbacks swim in the central Pacific. The cow banks gracefully steering her 12 m (40 ft) long body with the help of 4 m (13 ft) long pectoral flippers.

BRANDON D. COLE

A large female humpback whale protects her calf which swims above her. Beneath is a male humpback, escorting the pair.

The film team worked from a research boat that operated under special permission in its proximity to the whales.

DAVE RUDDICK

from the humpbacks. On board our boat we could scarcely believe what was happening - the idea of actually filming a humpback being attacked by orca was just too much to even dream about and yet it really looked as though it was about to happen. On the bow the cameraman Jeff Wayman peered anxiously towards the humpbacks.

Minutes passed, nothing happened. Eventually, and not entirely to my surprise, I saw the orca blow further down the sound, heading once more towards open water. Some of the humpbacks started to dive again. I wondered if they'd been trying to hide by keeping totally motionless. I also noticed

that two still appeared to be hugging the surface and checked on the radio with the other team to find out if anyone had filmed resting humpbacks. 'No',was the answer, so now that the predatory moment appeared to have passed, we decided to film five minutes of the 'sleeping' whales before heading after the orca again.

No sooner had we started filming than our skipper yelled out that the orca were breaching once again about half a mile away. Something looked strange about it, not the clean breaches you normally see. Checking through binoculars we saw to our amazement that it was a humpback breaching with

an orca firmly attached to his back! We raced after the action but by the time we arrived there was no longer any sign of the humpback - perhaps it had simply been too big for the small group of orca. Sometimes you look back on decisions and, with the wisdom of hindsight, kick yourself. But as I said to Geoff, "Okay, so we missed a world famous shot of orca predating 50 tonne humpbacks, but hey, at least we filmed a classic snoozing whale!" And all was not lost since later that day Rick filmed a great sequence of orca feeding on Dalls porpoise.

The humpback derives its name from its rudimentary dorsal fin.

Filming humpbacks from above has always presented a problem. The remote controlled airship made it possible to maintain a camera in position above the whales for prolonged periods without disturbing them.

Whales do not much care for noisy planes and helicopters so there are strict regulations over how close you can approach from the air. The aerial operation was the cue for one of my greater moments of cinematic madness. Collaborating with the brilliant remote model helicopter pilot and cameraman, Geoff Bell, I had decided that the answer to this problem lay with models. But we thought the very best solution would be a helium filled airship. We later discovered that an airship with enough lift to haul up even a tiny camera had to be over 8 m (25 ft) long - hardly a model!

In fact scientists had been dreaming of airships for ages, knowing that the best view of a whale was from the air. Their particular interest was in using an aerial platform to obtain scaled stills so they could measure the size of whales. But thinking about airships and actually creating a working machine are two hugely different things. It took all the genius that Geoff has in machining, designing and flying to pull this one off.

As we limped out to sea in a 3.5 m (11 ft) inflatable, gingerly towing a gossamer light 8 m (25 ft) airship over five miles offshore, I truly thought madness had set in. Who in their right mind would pick Alaska with its infamous weather and remoteness as their trial filming location? I think it's a sentiment that Flip Nicklin shared because during the few days that he joined us, his camera was happily clicking away at the mad

Brits in action. But the incredible airship actually worked. Once launched, no mean feat from a tiny bouncing zodiac, she just soared, even flying faster than our boat could manage at full throttle. Not only that, but the manoeuvrable airship, dubbed 'Byatt's Blimp' by the crew, would hover gently above the whales, remain airborne for an hour, and Geoff's magical remote camera system relayed pictures to us so that we could precisely frame the desired shots. Best of all the whales did not appear to notice it. It was tremendously exciting and our eccentric efforts not only produced great new whale footage, but also pioneered a new tool for research scientists.

The filming of *Whale* was really what wildlife filming should be all about. We took an extraordinary, though much filmed, animal and looked at it with new eyes and better understanding than ever before. The resulting film will open a new window on the world of humpbacks, hopefully influencing public opinion in favour of protecting both the whales themselves and their ocean environment. We developed some new techniques which enabled us to capture unique images and which will be used in future by scientists to advance our knowledge of whales. It was a privileged and rewarding assignment, and one that we shall never forget. Rick and I feel doubly privileged to be able to share our incredible experiences with millions of viewers throughout the world.

JIM DARLING

179

Humpback sounds at sunset.

Leviathan feeding frenzy - involving up to 20 whales, operating in a tight
bunch as they scoop herring into their jaws during 'bubble-net' feeding.

BRANDON D. COLE

BRANDON D. COLE

A vapourous cloud of exhaled breath hangs in the cool Alaskan air. Humpbacks have huge lung capacities and can hold their breath for at least half an hour.

Pectoral slapping - either as a method of communication or just for play, humpbacks create loud slaps by striking the water surface with their fins. The Latin name of the humpback, Megaptera novaengliae *means 'large-winged New Englander', an apt description, as this picture confirms.*

BRANDON D. COLE

BRANDON D. COLE

Humpback whale

Megaptera novaeangliae

GENERAL DESCRIPTION

Mid-size black baleen whale. Belly may be white. Has a pleated throat and up to 800 plates of baleen in its upper jaw. Its dorsal fin is small and commonly hooked. It has huge pectoral fins which may extend to a third of its body length. The pectorals are usually black and white on both sides and have heavily knobbed leading edges. Tail flukes, which are usually extended above the surface when the whale sounds, are notched and individually patterned with varying amounts of white. The flattened top of the head is covered with knobs, reminiscent of the surface of a dill pickle. Distinguishing features also include the extendible grooved throat and serpentine body, with huge wing-like flippers making the whale seem to fly through the water. Its latin name means 'big-winged New Englander'. Humpbacks grow to a length of 11 to 15 m (36-49 ft) and weigh up to 60 tonnes.

This is one of 11 species of baleen whales, the largest of the whales, all of which have a baleen filter in their mouth, to strain plankton and small fish from the sea; some pleating in the throat, to allow expansion for gulping; and a two-nostril opening at the blowhole, compared to the single one in toothed whales.

They issue a wide variety of calls ranging from grunts and screams, often emitted when feeding, to a complex breeding song consisting of a sequence of sounds, approximately 12-15 minutes long, that can be repeated for hours.

BRANDON D. COLE

BRANDON D. COLE

BREEDING and RAISING of YOUNG

Humpback whales breed in the sub-tropics during winter months, in regions such as Hawaii, Mexico, or the Caribbean. Courtship, which takes place between January and April, may involve a considerable number of males competing for one female. A single calf, 4 m (13 ft) in length, is born after a 10 to 11 months gestation period. The mother whale continues to provide milk to her offspring for up to a year. The young are more playful than adults, breaching and tail slapping repeatedly. Baleen whales are the fastest growing mammals on earth and humpback calves increase their weight between five and eight times during the first year.

MOVEMENT AND FEEDING

Most humpback whales migrate between subtropical breeding areas in winter and high latitude feeding grounds in summer. In the north Pacific there are three main breeding areas, Hawaii,

BRANDON D. COLE

Mexico and Japan with whales migrating between their winter areas and summer feeding grounds around the Pacific rim, from northern California to northern Japan. The primary destination of the Mexican population appears to be northern California, and the Hawaiian population, Alaska. Movements are not quite this predictable, however, since some whales may travel to a range of north Pacific destinations over several years with, for example, a whale found in Mexico one winter turning up in Hawaii the next. As an exception to the migration rule some whales apparently do not leave the feeding grounds during the winter. The south Pacific populations travel between the Antarctic and south Pacific islands.

The humpbacks' main diet is small fish and plankton. They feed either singly or in groups, gulping huge mouthfuls of water and prey, and then forcing the water through sieve-like baleen using their immense tongues. The sieved food is left trapped on the baleen and the humpback can then swallow it. Group feeding amongst humpbacks provides one of the most spectacular behavioural events in the animal kingdom. In this joint effort, one or more whales emits a circle or 'net' of bubbles as they slowly rise from a depth below their prey fish (herring or sand lance). The bubbles surround the fish which are frightened into a tight ball. As this happens the whole group of humpbacks lunge into the middle of their temporary 'net', gulping herring at the surface. Humpbacks may also eat mysids, krill, and other planktonic animals.

RESEARCH

The fact that humpbacks can be predictably found close to shore has allowed researchers to study this species more than any other baleen whale. Some of the first and most detailed descriptions of population definition, migrations, social organization, mating and feeding behaviour for any baleen whale have arisen from humpback studies. Today researchers are focusing on questions of population dynamics - birth rates, survival rates of calves and population growth models; ecology - especially the utilization of various prey species, and social behaviour to understand the social requirements of the species.

CONSERVATION

Humpback whales were hunted extensively world-wide until the mid-1960s, when only remnant populations remained in many regions. In 1966 they were given endangered species status and officially protected internationally, however large-scale illegal hunting did continue in some regions. Today many humpback populations appear to be recovering in different parts of the world, including the north Pacific, and there is optimism that this species' population could eventually return to its pre-whaling abundance. However some populations are still very small, and threats to habitat and food supply will play a major role in determining the humpback's future.

Filming Locations:
Hawaii
S.E. Alaska
Revillagigedo Archipelago, Mexico

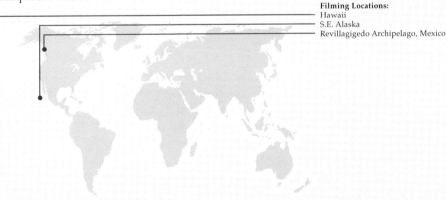

Appendix

The Contributors

DAVID ATTENBOROUGH, narrator and presenter of *The Wildlife Specials* and author of the foreword to this book, has enjoyed a distinguished career in broadcasting spanning more than 40 years. In 1954 he launched the first of his famous *Zoo Quest* series which, over the next 10 years, took him to the wilder parts of the world. In between times, his programmes included political broadcasts, archaeological quizzes, short stories, gardening and religious programmes.

In 1965, he was Controller of BBC-2 and became responsible for the introduction of colour television into Britain. In January 1969, he was appointed Director of Programmes with editorial responsibility for both the BBC's television networks. Then, in 1973, he resigned to return to programme-making. First came *Eastwards with Attenborough*, a natural history series set in south-east Asia, then *The Tribal Eye*, examining tribal art.

In 1979, he wrote and presented the 13-part series, *Life on Earth* - at the time the most ambitious series ever produced by the BBC Natural History Unit. In 1984 came its sequel, *The Living Planet*, and in 1990 followed the final part of the trilogy, *The Trials of Life*. He also wrote and presented two shorter series, *The First Eden*, on the Mediterranean,

and *Lost Worlds, Vanished Lives*, about fossils. In 1993, he presented the spectacular *Life in the Freezer*, a celebration of Antarctica. In 1995, he wrote and presented the epic *The Private Life of Plants*. Last year, *Attenborough in Paradise* fulfilled a lifelong ambition for David, to make a special film about the elusive but beautiful birds of paradise. He is currently working on a major 10-part series for the BBC, *The Life of Birds* to be broadcast in 1998.

In 1985, David Attenborough was knighted. Over the years he has received honorary degrees and a number of prestigious awards. He is a Trustee of the British Museum, and was also a Trustee of the Royal Botanic Gardens, Kew. He is President of the Royal Society for Nature Conservation.

KEITH SCHOLEY, series producer for *The Wildlife Specials*, was born in Tanzania and raised in East Africa until his teens. Following a B.Sc. degree in zoology at the University of Bristol he studied the aerodynamics of animal flight for a PhD at the same university. He also obtained a pilot's licence with the RAF University Air Squadron at this time. After research experience in Borneo, Peru, and Kenya he joined the BBC Natural History Unit in 1982, as a researcher on the David Attenborough series *The Living Planet*. As an assistant producer, he capitalised on his African origins,

working on Natural World programmes such as, *Leopard: A Darkness in the Grass* (1986) and *The Great Rift* (1989) and then, as a producer, he made a film about cheetahs for *Wildlife on One: The Haunted Huntress* 1990), and two programmes for *The Natural World* BBC television series: the first on African wild dogs (*Running for their Lives* 1990) and the second on the Ethiopian highlands (*Island in the Air* 1990). Later he contributed programmes about the relationship people have with Africa's largest resident, the elephant, to the series *Natural Neighbours* and *Dawn to Dusk*. He also played a part in the live production *Africa Watch* (1989) and from this experience developed and jointly produced *Big Cat Diary* (1996). A keen underwater naturalist, he has produced two marine wildlife films for *Wildlife on One, Malice in*

Wonderland (1994) and *Reef Encounter* (1997). Returning to his research interest in animal locomotion, he produced a mini-series for *The Natural World* about energy, called *Prisoner's of the Sun* (1992).

In 1993 he became one of the producers on David Attenborough's series *The Private Life of Plants* and in 1994 was appointed as editor of *Wildlife on One*. Here, he also oversaw other projects like the Nature Special *Tiger Crisis* and the Wildlife Special *Great White Shark*. He is currently running a series of Wildlife Specials and commencing production of the millennium series about biodiversity, *The State of the Planet*.

Awards for the programmes he has worked on include Emmies, Aces, Wildscreen Pandas, Jackson Hole awards and nominations for BAFTA and the RTS.

AMANDA BARRETT's career in wildlife film-making began in a relatively unorthodox manner with a degree from Bristol University in Ancient Mediterranean Studies. She started work in the Natural History Unit as a secretary to the Head of Natural History Development. Research work for a variety of programmes, both natural history and documen-taries, led her to a chance meeting with Owen Newman during filming for *The Great Rift*. Since then she and Owen have produced several films including *Firebird*, *A Graze with Danger*, *Night of the Leopard* and the award winning *Lions - Pride in Peril*.

ANDY BYATT began work with the Natural History Unit in 1989 as a safety diver for *The Natural World: Splashdown*. That experience led to production work as a researcher for *The Really Wild Show*. He spent three years researching, directing and producing children's programmes for the BBC Natural History Unit. Film credits include a number of *Wildlife on One* programmes, including the award-winning film on jellyfish, *The Swarm*; *The Besieged - War of the Termites*; and two films in the *Incredible Journeys* series: *A Rattlesnake's Tale* and *A Whale's Voyage*. Andy has a wide interest in natural history filming and is a skilled diver.

MICHAEL RICHARDS qualified at Guildford School of Art as a stills photographer and went straight to the Royal Society for the Protection of Birds to work within their film unit. In 1980 he made his first 50 minute film: *Where Eagles Fly* about the golden eagle in Scotland. After four years with the unit he turned freelance. He now has over 50 credits from films made for the BBC as well as other organisations, including Survival Anglia. *Goshawk - Phantom of the Forest* was made with Hugh Miles and more recently he produced and filmed *Harris Hawks - Wolves of the Air* for *National Geographic Explorer*. His last four films have all been for the BBC's *Wildlife on One*.

KAREN BASS's wildlife film-making career began in the Natural History Unit working with David Attenborough on *The First Eden*, a series about the Mediterranean. She went on to direct *Brockside* - a Christmas special about urban badgers, and the series *The Birth of Europe*. As a producer, her award-winning films for *The Natural World*, *Toadskin Spell* and *Monkey in the Mirror*, took her to all corners of the world to film frogs and primates.
Wildlife on One credits include the award winning *Back Street Bandits* about urban racoons, *Possums - Tales of the Unexpected*, *Bat eared Fox*, and *Pygmy Chimp - The Last Great Ape*, a touching portrait of man's closest relatives in the jungles of America. She is currently working on a new series about South American wildlife.

MARTHA HOLMES, producer of *Polar Bear*, first specialised in marine biology and gained her PhD in York studying the behaviour of tropical fish. She started work with BBC television presenting programmes such as *Reefwatch*, a live underwater broadcast from the northern Red Sea, then *Splashdown* which was followed by the award-winning wildlife-adventure series *Sea Trek*. She worked in Antarctica for David Attenborough's *Life in the Freezer* and has more recently produced a number of other natural history films including *Hippos Out of Water*, *Being There - Antarctica*, *Deadly Liaisons*, and *Otters - the Truth*. She is currently involved with the production of a major new series about the world's oceans which is due for release around the turn of the century.

MIKE SALISBURY, producer of *Wolf*, has been working at the BBC Natural History Unit for over twenty years. He has worked with David Attenborough on *Life On Earth* and was executive producer of *Lost Worlds - Vanished Lives*. He co-produced *The Discovery of Animal Behaviour* and has produced many films for *Wildlife on One* and *The Natural World*, including the award winners *Through Animal Eyes* and *Kingdom of the Ice Bear*. For three years Mike was editor of *The Natural World* series, a post he relinquished to become executive producer of *The Private Life Of Plants*. Mike's considerable experience of wildlife film production is now being brought to bear on the production of David Attenborough's next major series *The Life Of Birds*.

Acknowledgements

THE WILDLIFE SPECIALS is based on six natural history programmes made by the BBC Natural History Unit and narrated by Sir David Attenborough. The Series Producer was Keith Scholey, and individual programmes were produced by: Martha Holmes, POLAR BEAR; Mike Salisbury, WOLF; Karen Bass, CROCODILE; Amanda Barrett and Owen Newman, LEOPARD; John Downer, EAGLE; Andy Byatt and Rick Rosenthal, WHALE.

Invaluable production support was given by the following people: Ruth Flowers, Production Manager; Nicky Spode and Felicity Mudge, Unit Managers and Sharon Thomas, Production Secretary.

The team on POLAR BEAR: Principal Cameraman: Doug Allan. Additional Photography: Martin Saunders, Piers Finzel and Hitesh Makan. Technical Filming Assistance: Peter Scoones. Scientific Consultants: Ian Stirling, Andy Derocher, Malcolm Ramsay, Øystein Wiig, Mitch Taylor. Field Assistance: Mats Forsberg, Jason Roberts, Isaac Shooyook, Don Moors, Joe Kaludjak, Geir Aasebøstøl, Arne Kristoffersen, Bonnie Chartier. Additional Support: Joseph Renson. Production Co-ordinator: Philippa Lawson. Film Editor: Jo Payne. Dubbing Editor: Lucy Rutherford.

The team on WOLF: Principal Cameraman: Ian MacCarthy. Additional Photography: Jeff Turner, Justine Evans. Sound Recordist: Trevor Gosling. Scientific Consultants: Ludwig Carbyn, L. David Mech, Christoph Promberger, Ovidu Ionescu, Satish Kumbar, Jenny Ryon. Field Assistance: Tom Clarke, Anton Pauw. Assistant Producer: Michelle Thompson. Production Co-ordinator: Anne Holmes. Film Editor: Martin Elsbury. Dubbing Editor: Angela Groves. Music: Ian Butcher, Steven Faux.

The team on CROCODILE: Researcher: Gavin Maxwell. Principal Cameraman: Richard Kirby. Additional Photography: Daniel Christen, Martin Dohrn, Peter Scoones, Kim Wolhuter. Programme Consultant: Tony Pooley. Scientific Advisors: Dave Blake, John Thorbjarnarson, Kent Vliet, Tim Williams. Production Co-ordinator: Fiona Marsh. Editor: Tim Coope. Dubbing Editor: Lucy Rutherford.

The team on LEOPARD: Camera & Sound: Owen Newman. Technical Assistance: Vernon Baillie. Much additional support in Zambia was provided by: Celia Krige and her family, Penny Lapper, Jason Alfonsin, Xen Vlahakis, Akim Mweynya, Edwin Matokwani, Nassan Tembo and the Mfuwe rangers, Philip Berry, Ian Salisbury, Charl Beukes, Derek Shenton, Alex Stassino, Jake da Motta, Nick Aslin, Pam McKinstry, Jo and Robin Pope. In Namibia, the team was assisted by Philip Stander, Philippa Haden, the Ju/Hoan bushmen, Tsumkwe Conservation Trust, Allan Cilliers and Eugene Marais. Production Co-ordinators: Philippa Lawson, Liz Appleby, Clare Flegg. Researcher: Marguerite Smits Van Oyen. Editor: Stuart Napier. Dubbing Editor: Lucy Rutherford.

The team on EAGLE: Cameraman: Michael W. Richards. Assistant Producer: Neil Lucas. Researcher: Gavin Maxwell. Production Co-ordinator: Cathi Beloe. Editor: Stuart Napier. Dubbing Editor: Paul Cowgill. Script Consultant: Jeff Watson.

The team on WHALE: Principal Cameraman: Rick Rosenthal. Additional Photography: Shane Moore, Jeff Wayman, Geoff Bell. Sound Recordist: David Ruddick. Scientific Consultant & Script Advisor: Dr Jim Darling. Scientific Advisor: Professor Bruce Mate. Additional Support: Jim Barnes, Jim Eastwood, Chris Tulloch, Louis Rzen. Production Co-ordinator: Fiona Marsh. Film Editor: Dave Dickie. Dubbing Editor: Kate Hopkins. Composer: Roger Bolton.

The BBC Natural History Unit

The BBC Natural History Unit was established in 1957 and has grown to become the largest and most famous centre for natural history broadcasting in the world. Under its roof more than 100 production staff create about 180 television and radio programmes each year and the Unit's librarians manage a comprehensive archive of natural history films, tapes and sound recordings.

The Unit traces its roots back to work by some of this century's pioneering naturalists and broadcasters: people like Desmond Hawkins who produced the BBC's first natural history radio programmes in 1946; Peter Scott whose 1955 television series, *Look*, captured the imaginations of an entire generation of young naturalists, and who played an important role in later natural history programme making; Eric Ashby who revealed the secret lives of badgers to a fascinated public; Heinz Sielman

who probed the inside of a woodpecker's nest and Ronald Eastman who gave armchair naturalists a minnow's-eye view of a kingfisher fishing.

The Unit provided a focus for the developing talents of wildlife film-makers and naturalists, attracting wildlife presenters such as David Attenborough, Gerald Durrell, Jacques Yves-Cousteau, Desmond Morris, Tony Soper and David Bellamy; and resulting in long-running nature series such as *The World About Us* (1967), *Wildlife on One* (1977) and *The Natural World* (1983).

Life on Earth, a wildlife blockbuster researched, written and presented by David Attenborough, has been watched by over 500 million people in over 100 countries, creating a staggering impact on the general public's perception of wildlife. This hugely successful series of 13 programmes was followed by a number of other major series including *The Living Planet* (1984), *Trials of Life*

(1990) and *The Private Life of Plants* (1995). At the time of writing Sir David Attenborough is working on a new series about our planet's bird-life.

The Natural History Film Unit continues to push back new frontiers of wildlife film-making, creating ever more impressive wildlife programmes, drawing on the dedicated talents of some of the world's top cameramen and producers. In doing so it has reflected a growing concern for the welfare of our planet, first by showing the wealth and beauty of our wildlife, and second by drawing attention to its fragility and vulnerability.

The NHU has adopted new technologies that form part of the communications revolution, enabling it to maintain its position at the forefront of wildlife film-making. *The Wildlife Specials* are an example of the unit's commitment to high quality programmes that reveal new aspects of natural history, never before seen on television.

The NHU Picture Library

The majority of the photographs in this book were kindly provided by the NHU Picture Library, which is a valuable photographic resource, both for natural history publishers and researchers. It was established in 1995 in order to represent the work of top wildlife photographers from around the world and coordinate

stills relating to the Unit's filming activities. The rapidly expanding collection covers all aspects of the natural world including animal behaviour, wild plants, marine life, landscapes and environmental issues. The library also has a unique collection of stills on wildlife filming. Enquiries may be directed to the library's manager.

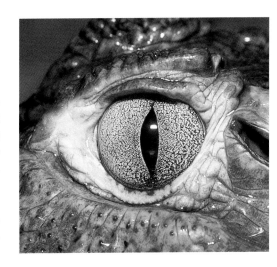

BBC Natural History Unit Picture Library, Broadcasting House, Whiteladies Road, Bristol, BS8 2LR. Tel: 0117 9746720 or 9732211. Fax: 0117 9238166. email: nhu.picture.library@bbc.co.uk. Manager: Helen Gilks.

Index